"*It's Okay Not to Be Okay* breathes fresh life on the arresting splendor of God's grace. Sheila speaks from a place of victory, grounded in the knowledge that we are meant to walk 'side by side with Jesus, learning to live freely and lightly.' Her encouragement and practical guidance will provide the tools you need to start again, discovering that through Christ you are always enough."

Lisa Bevere, *New York Times* bestselling author and
cofounder of Messenger International

"This may look like a book, but it's actually a bit of a personal life-saver that will feel like actual relief. Sheila Walsh doesn't merely write words, she lives her words—and the Word. When things honestly aren't okay, I don't know a wiser, more life-giving, Jesus-clinging guide than Sheila Walsh."

Ann Voskamp, *New York Times* bestselling author of
The Broken Way and *One Thousand Gifts*

"In this powerful book, Sheila shares the transforming truth that life is a process and that God never leaves nor forsakes us. There are rarely quick fixes in life, but Jesus offers us hope, healing, and wholeness. Okay doesn't live here, but Jesus does."

Christine Caine, founder of A21 and Propel Women

"*It's Okay Not to Be Okay* is a beautifully practical way forward through the ache of feeling not-enough. Sheila reminds us that God is so near and willing to meet us in our deepest places of weakness and hurt."

Jennie Allen, author of *Nothing to Prove* and founder
and visionary of the IF:Gathering

"A friend once told me that people aren't interested in what we got right nearly as much as how we've experienced divine redemption when we got it wrong. Sheila is always refreshingly transparent about where she's gotten it wrong so as to make Jesus the sole hero of her story. Her newest book, *It's Okay Not to Be Okay*, is a deeply encouraging—quite possibly transformative—tome for stumbling saints!"

Lisa Harper, bestselling author and Bible teacher

"Sheila Walsh's characteristic wisdom and encouragement shine in her newest book, *It's Okay Not to Be Okay*. Through personal stories and teachings from the Bible, Sheila shows us that it's okay to fail, as long as we get back up again—a life lesson I've tried to teach our children and to live out myself. After reading this book, you'll be equipped and inspired to strive for more."

Korie Robertson, author of Strong and Kind: Raising Kids of
Character and star of Duck Dynasty

"Life's moments, good and bad, come in waves. Sometimes during those tough moments, we need encouraging and uplifting words to feed our soul. In *It's Okay Not to Be Okay*, Sheila Walsh shares her stories and wisdom to encourage us to start afresh and move forward one step at a time. This book reminds us that even in those dark moments, God's light is there waiting at the end of the storm."

Roma Downey, producer, actor, and
New York Times bestselling author

"I have had the personal pleasure of knowing Sheila for a number of years now, and in that time have only known her to be a stunning example of grace and possibilities. Whilst tenacious and strong in spirit, she carries a softness and vulnerability that allows both her story and her take on life to resonate with all who come in contact with her. I am confident that her latest book, *It's Okay Not to Be Okay*, will point people to Christ and draw them onwards because of its raw, honest, and genuine nature."

Bobbie Houston, global co-senior pastor, Hillsong Church

"If you're struggling, if you're weary, if you're not okay—this book is for you. In these pages, Sheila Walsh reminds us that Christ doesn't look at our failures, only at how much we love him. Pick up this book for encouragement and inspiration to keep moving forward."

Mark Batterson, *New York Times* bestselling author
of *The Circle Maker* and lead pastor,
National Community Church

"In the twenty years of Women of Faith, Sheila shared the reality of her struggles year after year, giving millions of women hope and help and healing. Her message was consistently that it is okay with Jesus to not be okay. Now she has put all that she has been through and all that she has learned into this, her most powerful, most helpful, and most hopeful book yet, with the title of her consistent life message, 'It's Okay Not to Be Okay.' There is no finer communicator than Sheila Walsh in person or in print. If you have ever loved hearing her or reading anything by her, you will want this, her best book yet. If you have never read anything by her, start here. If you don't like it, if you don't find it powerful and inspirational, let me know, and I will give you your money back out of my own pocket. Yep, that's how badly I want you to read *It's Okay Not to Be Okay*."

Steve Arterburn, founder and chairman of *New Life
Live!* radio broadcast and bestselling author

"Are you aching for a second chance? Take a deep breath and read Sheila Walsh's new book! God will meet you in the fast-turning pages."

Karen Kingsbury, #1 *New York Times* bestselling
author of *To the Moon and Back*

"Here's the breakthrough you've been longing for! Let my friend Sheila Walsh help you escape the shackles that keep you down by finding grace and hope through Christ. Never underestimate the potential of YOU once you're empowered by the God who knows all of you and loves you completely!"

Lee Strobel, bestselling author of *The Case for Christ* and *The Case for Miracles*

"Sheila Walsh writes from deep within her soul and touches lives like few people I know. *It's Okay Not to Be Okay* is a call to celebrate our identity and victory in Christ and move forward with faith and freedom. As her pastor and friend, I recommend the book wholeheartedly."

Jack Graham, pastor, Prestonwood Baptist Church

it's okay
NOT TO BE OKAY

it's okay

NOT TO BE OKAY

Moving Forward
One Day at a Time

SHEILA WALSH

BakerBooks

a division of Baker Publishing Group
Grand Rapids, Michigan

© 2018 by Sheila Walsh

Published by Baker Books
a division of Baker Publishing Group
PO Box 6287, Grand Rapids, MI 49516-6287
www.bakerbooks.com

Paperback edition published 2019
ISBN 978-0-8010-9466-8

Printed in the United States of America

The Library of Congress has cataloged the original edition as follows:
Names: Walsh, Sheila, 1956– author.
Title: It's okay not to be okay : moving forward one day at a time / Sheila Walsh.
Description: Grand Rapids : Baker Publishing Group, 2018. | Includes bibliographical
    references.
Identifiers: LCCN 2018016838 | ISBN 9780801078002 (cloth)
Subjects: LCSH: Christian women—Religious life. | Regret—Religious aspects—Christianity. |
    Change (Psychology)—Religious aspects—Christianity.
Classification: LCC BV4527 .W3543 2018 | DDC 248.8/43—dc23
LC record available at https://lccn.loc.gov/2018016838

ITPE ISBN: 978-0-8010-7801-9

In keeping with biblical principles of creation stewardship, Baker Publishing Group advocates the responsible use of our natural resources. As a member of the Green Press Initiative, our company uses recycled paper when possible. The text paper of this book is composed in part of post-consumer waste.

19 20 21 22 23 24 25   7 6 5 4 3 2 1

This book is dedicated with love and admiration to every weary soul who falls down and gets back up, over and over again. It's easy to fall; it takes courage to rise up and take the next step.

Contents

Introduction

It's Okay Not to Be Okay

I wish I could take my twenty-one-year-old (recovering-from-teenage-acne) face in my hands and tell her, "It's okay not to be okay, I promise." Would she have believed me? I don't think so. She was determined to get everything right.

It started with a photograph. I was cleaning out drawers the other day and found an old photograph under a roll of Christmas paper. I sat down on the sofa and studied the picture. I'm in a white dress and a graduation gown, twenty-one years old, graduating from seminary. My hair is short and dark. It had taken about three years to recover from my experiment with a perm that left me looking like a pack of dogs had assumed my hair was lunch. In the photograph I'm smiling, confident, ready to take on the world for Jesus.

My heart aches. There's so much I'd like to tell her.

"Moisturize your neck! You'll thank me later!"

If I had only ten minutes, I'd cut to the chase. I'd tell her this will not be the life she imagined. I'd tell her that she will disappoint people and they will disappoint her, but she'll learn from it. I'd let her know that she'll fall down over and over again, but rather than understanding the love of God less she'll get it more. I'd let her know her heart is going to break, but she'll survive and it will change how she sees people, not as causes to be saved but as people to be loved. I'd let her know that sometimes the night will get very dark, but she will never be alone even when she's absolutely convinced she is. I'd let her know that she's loved. I'd tell her to get rid of her punishing list of things she thinks she needs to get right.

I lived so much of my life with a list of things to change, to do better—if not on paper then in my mind. I think most of us do, and the message is always the same: we can do better.

We'll not only join the gym, we'll go!

This new diet plan will work and by summer we'll be bikini ready. (Note to self: don't you dare buy a bikini. Even if you're thinner, things are not where they used to be and no one but your loving husband needs to know that.)

We'll start that read-through-the-Bible-in-a-year plan again. (Last year I got to May 7 and got distracted, and by the time I realized it, I was a whole Leviticus, fifty-three Psalms, and Romans behind.)

We'll recover from the overspending and be financially responsible.

We'll cook wholesome, nutritious meals for our family and sit down at least five nights a week together at the table.

We'll reduce our television watching and read more books.

But sometimes the messages carry much more weight.

This marriage will work.

We will get out of debt.

Our children will come back to Christ.

We'll eat better to save our lives not our waistlines.

I don't know what your internal list looks like, but if it's anything like mine it usually serves to let us know where we've failed. Lists are written when the kids are asleep or you've had a good night's sleep and a cup of coffee. The trouble is, the kids wake up and that impossible woman you work with gets louder and more obnoxious by the minute and no amount of coffee is going to help.

And what about our spiritual lives? That can be the most judgmental list of all. When we assume that God's love is based on our behavior we've set ourselves up for a devastating fall.

I'll pray more.

I'll share my faith at work.

I'll read my Bible from Genesis to the maps in the back of the book.

I'll trust God without questioning.

So, why did I title this book *It's Okay Not to Be Okay?* These words might sound a bit like a bumper sticker to you, but they don't to me. I want you to know that these words were fought for. They could sound like the waving of a white flag, six words of surrender, but they're not.

For me they are words of victory!

I've let go of beating myself up trying to live a life that Jesus never asked me to live. The life my "fresh out of seminary, determined to save the world, to love the unlovely, get nine hours of sleep every night and never let God down" self tried to live for so long.

I don't know where you're at in life as you read this, but if I could sit down with you for a while, I'd say, "Take a deep breath in and hold it for five seconds, and then let it out. Again. Again."

Then I'd tell you that it *really* is okay not to be okay. That's why Jesus came.

I gave my life to Him when I was eleven years old. As I write, I'm sixty-one. That's fifty years of falling down and getting back up. Fifty years of trying to be worth loving. Fifty years of doing the same things over and over, hoping they'd turn out differently this time. (Yes, I do know that's the definition of insanity.)

Here's the great news: It's also fifty years of the faithfulness of God and this beautiful invitation from Christ:

Are you tired? Worn out? Burned out on religion? Come to me. Get away with me and you'll recover your life. I'll show you how to take a real rest. Walk with me and work with me—watch how I do it.

15

Learn the unforced rhythms of grace. I won't lay anything heavy or ill-fitting on you. Keep company with me and you'll learn to live freely and lightly. (Matt. 11:28–30 Message)

What a lovely place to start again, side by side with Jesus, learning to live freely and lightly.

I read an old Chinese proverb that said, "The best time to plant a tree was twenty years ago. The second-best time is now."

I like that. Those are hope-filled words. They say that we get to start again and again and again. No matter what's true in your life at this moment, I want to remind you that God loves you, right now, no matter what's going on around or inside you. These words may fall flat for you right now if you find yourself in an unfamiliar place, a difficult season.

Perhaps you're facing the end of a marriage and you either feel like a failure or that you've been betrayed and abandoned.

You may be facing an empty nest and have no idea what your life should revolve around now.

Perhaps you have lost a loved one and the very idea of moving forward not only seems impossible, it feels wrong.

You may think, *I've done this before. I've tried to start again and it didn't work.*

Or perhaps, if you're honest, you are just too tired to try. I understand that. I've been there.

I'd like to simply say, gently, you were made for more. You are worth fighting for. Christ thought you were worth dying for. Would you be willing to open your heart to the possibility of moving forward, one day at a time?

Life rarely offers quick fixes; it's a process, and God is in it with us, all the way. He doesn't look for perfection in us; He sees that in Christ. You don't need to be okay because Jesus has made you all right. He's paid the bill in full. He's covered our "not okay-ness." Okay doesn't live here, but Jesus does. All He looks for in us is a willingness to take the next step.

Okay doesn't live here,
but Jesus does.

All He looks for in us
is a *willingness*
to take the next step.

one

Take the First Step

My health may fail, and my spirit may grow weak,
but God remains the strength of my heart;
he is mine forever.

—Psalm 73:26

Forever—is composed of Nows.

—Emily Dickinson

It was 10 PM. Not too late by normal standards, but late if you've been up several times through the night for the past ten nights. I was trying to get settled in bed. Trying to relax a bit and watch the women's freestyle ice skating competition, but the TV signal had just gone out . . . again. I was about ready to throw the remote through the screen. My husband, Barry, was exhausted and snoring like he was the one in a competition and was clearly in the lead. I thought about giving him a gentle nudge, but I didn't have the heart to wake him. He'd been sleeping on the sofa downstairs for the past ten nights, so to be back in our bed was bliss. Now, before you begin to assume anything or pray for us, we didn't have marital issues. Our twenty-one-year-old son was home from college and had just had his tonsils and adenoids removed. He was in a lot of pain.

The doctor told us this was the most painful surgery an adult can have, but it was worse than we imagined. On the day of his surgery I made the mistake of asking Christian to open his mouth so that I could have a look inside before I drove his semi-conscious self home.

Christian pulled down the visor on the passenger side and looked first. He turned his big brown eyes toward me, clearly shocked. "Oh my gosh, Mom, look at this!"

Wow! You can't un-see some things. It looked as if the surgeon took a garden trowel and dug two gaping holes in the back of his throat.

"Yeah, that's . . . well, wow . . . okay . . . hmm . . . Let's get you home," I said.

The first three days were rough, but when we hit day four, his pain went to a whole new level. He was literally shaking from the pain. He couldn't eat, and it hurt to drink. It was hard for him to swallow anything. I had to put his pain pills in Jell-O so they would slip down easier. The doctor told us to be vigilant about staying on top of the pain and make sure he took his pills on time, so I set my alarm for midnight, 4 AM, and 8 AM. Barry slept downstairs on the sofa outside of his bedroom in case he needed anything during the night. Now we were on day ten and things were finally beginning to look up.

I turned the television off, waited ten seconds, and turned it on again. Nothing. I was tired but wide awake, so I went downstairs to make a cup of tea. I checked in on Christian while the water was boiling, and he was fast asleep. It was a welcome sight. There are so many things we take for granted until they're absent, like the simple gift of your child sleeping through the night. I thought of the families who have chronically ill children. How do they cope?

I can't imagine. I paused in the kitchen and prayed for moms and dads who long for a break after ten days but instead the days turn into weeks and months.

I was beginning to feel as if I could fall asleep, so I went back upstairs and climbed into bed. It was then that I became uncomfortably aware of a damp spot beneath me. I gingerly put my hand out and discovered not a spot but a puddle and one sheepish looking dog. Belle, our Bichon Frise who sleeps on our bed, is fourteen years old, and the thoughts *I need to go to the bathroom* and *I just went to the bathroom* now seem to occur at exactly the same time. The vet told us we need to put her in diapers at night, but with everything else going on I'd forgotten. Now came the interesting part, trying to diaper a reluctant dog in the dark. I would get half of it on and she'd take off across the bed. At one point, I realized I was diapering her head. Finally, I had her pinned down and the diaper on, when the television suddenly came blaring on. Barry shot up in alarm just as I fell out of bed. I sat on the floor beside the bed and started to cry.

Have you ever had one of those days when you've just had enough? If you have to do one more load of laundry or find one more recipe for chicken or take one more kid to a sports practice you might just physically combust. What I went through in those few days was nothing compared to what many women have to face, but I felt overwhelmed and had had enough. I think of a dear friend. What she deals with on a daily basis is hard for me to imagine. She is wheelchair bound and has to rely on others for everything. She has no family where she lives, and she is dependent on local health workers to bathe her, bring her food, and every other thing that I can do by myself without thinking about it. She, like me, and like you I imagine, wants to live a life that's honoring to God, and yet she's told me sometimes it feels as if it's not enough, that *she's* not enough.

As I sat on the floor that night feeling sorry for myself, I was tired. I'd overeaten since I'd been up during the night, I'd had to cancel my appointment at the hair salon to get my roots done and was beginning to resemble a skunk, and, once more, I was behind in my Bible study plan. I was disappointed in myself and discouraged. All I wanted to do was get Christian's post-surgery ice cream out of the freezer and consume the whole thing. I think what discouraged me the most was the feeling of being back in the same place—again.

You see, somewhere deep inside, although I'd never admit this to anyone but you, I think I can be Super Woman. I'm too old for the tights, but the rest works. I want to be the best mom in the world. I want to be the best wife in the world. I want to honor God with every thought and every action, and I just don't. Some days I'm very aware of God's presence, and prayer and thanksgiving flow easily. Other days I open my Bible and it seems dry and prayer is hard work. I have a habit of stretching myself too thin. I want to say yes to everything and be a superhero for God.

I don't think I'm alone. I've talked to lots of women who feel let down by their lives; it's a common thread. Here's my question though: Are we discouraged because of the unrealistic expectations we put on ourselves—expecting ourselves to be what God never designed us to be? Think about it for a moment. How many times do you feel like you're not enough? It makes me wonder where we got the idea of what "enough" is. Take a typical Sunday morning: You finally get everyone ready for church, into the car, dropped off at their various classes, and flop down in your seat. At first, it's hard to enter in to the worship because of a million other things going through your head, but eventually you feel the presence of God and you focus your heart and mind. The message that morning seems to be tailor-made for you. Every Scripture speaks to you, and you leave encouraged. You remember who you really are; you're not just Sam's mom or David's wife. You are a child of God and you are loved. On the drive home, you even think up one more way to cook chicken. And then Monday comes.

Monday-Morning Jesus

What happens between Sunday and Monday? Why does it feel like Monday-morning Jesus is not as clear and present sometimes as Sunday-morning Jesus? When we leave the service on Sunday, we believe certain things to be true:

I am a child of God.

God loves me just as I am.

All things work together for good to those who love God.

God is for me.

My prayers matter.

Yet, as we move into the week, it's harder to believe that God loves us just as we are because, honestly, we don't love ourselves just as we are. There are always things we want to change about ourselves. We compare ourselves to other moms in the carpool line or at work, and we don't always come off well.

I remember Christian's first morning in second grade after we'd just moved to Dallas. I went into his classroom with all the other moms and saw that several of them were in little tennis skirts with tanned and toned legs. My legs haven't been tanned or toned since . . . well . . . never mind. One mom introduced herself to me and gave me a card (I kid you not) for Dallas's best plastic surgeon. I remember muttering something like, if I'm ever in a car accident, I'll call. Crazy stuff! Most situations are not that extreme, but I think we all do it. We compare ourselves to what we see in others, and when we do we think that we'll never be enough. What we need to remember, though, is that other women are comparing themselves to others too. It's a vicious game of smoke and mirrors and no one wins.

What about believing that all things work together for good to those who love God? What happens to that when something really hard hits your family? How can what's happening right now be good? It's hard not to ask that question in the back of your mind: Is God really listening to my prayers, because nothing seems to be changing?

Perhaps your situation is even harder than that. You don't even feel God's presence in church. Maybe you stopped going because of something someone said to you, or you look at everyone else around you who seems to be "getting it," and you, if you're honest, don't. You may have talked about something you're struggling with in a small group, and you could tell by the reactions of others that they were shocked. Now they look at you differently. That's a very lonely, isolating place to be.

I want to say something loud and clear in the first chapter: it's okay not to be okay! The bottom line is that we were never designed to be everything to everyone. Life is hard, and we all face problems. Those who say they don't have any problems are doing one of two things:

1. Hiding their problems
2. Pretending they don't have any

I'll get back to that in a moment.

I want to be clear that this is not a self-help, feel-good-about-yourself book. That might help for a moment, but when the first storm hits every word would vanish like the morning mist. What I want us to look at is this: What does God say about who we are? Does God expect us to have it all together, and why do we always feel that there's something not quite right with everything?

For that we'll have to take a look back in our history—way, way back.

Plan A

The LORD God caused the man to fall into a deep sleep. While the man slept, the LORD God took out one of the man's ribs and closed up the opening. Then the LORD God made a woman from the rib, and he brought her to the man.

"At last!" the man exclaimed.

> "This one is bone from my bone,
>   and flesh from my flesh!
> She will be called 'woman,'
>   because she was taken from 'man.'"

This explains why a man leaves his father and mother and is joined to his wife, and the two are united into one.

Now the man and his wife were both naked, but they felt no shame. (Gen. 2:21–25)

Genesis 2 describes the creation of Adam and Eve. It's hard to relate to, because we've never experienced that kind of perfect life. They were naked but they felt no shame. This is way more than Adam and Eve feeling good about skinny-dipping in the Garden. This is the way things were always meant to be. There were no barriers between them and God. They were naked in their emotions.

No shame.

No fear.

No guilt.

No questioning.

No comparing.

No sickness.

Then everything changed. When they rebelled against God's instruction to eat from any tree in the garden apart from the Tree of Knowledge of Good and Evil, life as they knew it was shattered. In Genesis 3:7 we read, "At that moment their eyes were opened, and they suddenly felt shame at their nakedness. So they sewed fig leaves together to cover themselves." The story continues in verse 10 when God asks Adam where he is: "He replied, 'I heard you walking in the garden, so I hid. I was afraid because I was naked.'"

There you have it!

Shame.

Fear.

Covering up.

Hiding.

. . . and we've been doing it ever since.

From that day on there has never been a man or woman born who doesn't have to contend with these emotions. They are the legacy of plan B.

I believe (and this is my belief alone) that something of the DNA of Eden runs deep in us.

We know things should be different.

We know we should be better.

We know life should be fair.

We know that death is wrong.

We know that something is wrong with everything and we try to fix it. The truth is, we can't.

That's why Christ, the second Adam, came. When Christ came, He didn't come to return earth to Eden at His birth. He came to pay the price for our rebellion and sin and make it possible for you and me, through faith in Christ, to spend eternity with Him. Then everything that was lost will be restored. Here's a sneak preview of the greatest upcoming attraction:

Then I saw a new heaven and a new earth, for the old heaven and the old earth had disappeared. And the sea was also gone. And I saw the holy city, the new Jerusalem, coming down from God out of heaven like a bride beautifully dressed for her husband.

I heard a loud shout from the throne, saying, "Look, God's home is now among his people! He will live with them, and they will be his people. God himself will be with them. He will wipe every tear from their eyes, and there will be no more death or sorrow or crying or pain. All these things are gone forever." (Rev. 21:1–4)

That will be a day like no other. No more death or suffering. No more cancer or disease. No more broken relationships and broken hearts. All these things will be gone forever. Hallelujah!

But, we're not there yet. We're living in the aftermath of the fall and that is hard. It is also important to remember that's where we are.

It's okay not to be okay because we're not home yet.

It's okay not to be enough because God doesn't ask us to be.

What He wants is to move in—to move into our hearts and our homes, our minds and our struggles. Jesus is not a hashtag to add on to your life. He wants to be your everything.

#Jesus

I lived a good part of my life adding Jesus on as a hashtag. I didn't mean to. I didn't know I was doing it, but I was. Whether I was dealing with loss, or depression, or financial or relational struggles, I did my best to fix things. I tried to do better and then asked Jesus to help me. It was as if prayer was an add-on and Christ was only involved once I'd given it my best shot. This is not how we are designed to live in plan B. Even the great apostle Paul struggled to grasp this.

In 2 Corinthians 12, Paul talks about a miraculous experience he had with God where he was caught up into another world, which he calls paradise. That word, *paradise*, comes from a Persian word meaning "a walled-garden." When a Persian king wanted to convey a great honor on a man or woman he would invite them to walk in the garden with him. It's a lovely picture of a very intimate time that Paul had with God. Perhaps Paul had a glimpse into what plan A was like, or perhaps he viewed our coming glory, but it was only for a time. Then he goes on to write about returning to the reality of plan B.

He continues to write in chapter 12 about a "thorn in the flesh" that he was struggling with. Theologians over the ages have debated what Paul's thorn was. For us here, the answer to that is not important. What matters is what God told Paul.

> Three different times I begged the Lord to take it away. Each time he said, "My grace is all you need. My power works best in weakness." (2 Cor. 12:8–9)

Paul is weak. He is not enough. He's in pain and he's asking God to fix it, to take away the weakness. God says no. Then God says these two things:

My grace is all you need.

My power works best in weakness.

The word *skolops* used in this passage can be translated as "thorn" but just as likely as "stake." The image of a stake is one of something driven straight into the heart. Whatever it was, it cost Paul dearly. So here we have a man who had been blinded by a vision of the risen Christ (Acts 9:3–4), had been used to see countless men and women saved, and had been given the gift of a vision from God so great, so above our understanding, that he was not able to talk about it. Yet here he opened his heart to us and let us know, *I'm not okay, I'm not enough.*

God's answer to Paul is His answer to us.

My grace is sufficient; it's enough for you.

My strength works best in weakness.

What is grace? We sing about it, we say it before meals, but what is the grace of God? How does it meet our *not enough-ness?* Grace is a gift unique to those in relationship with God. No other religion offers grace.

I was in Cambodia recently working to rescue girls caught in sex trafficking and took a picture that showed the profound difference between our loving God who, in Christ, became a baby—literally took on a human shoe size—and the gods of Southeast Asia. I had been working that morning in the worst slum I've ever been in. The people there live in broken-down shacks over a garbage dump. When the sun shines the stench is almost unbearable. I stepped outside to take a breath of air and saw that the slum was right beside a huge, ornate, recently built temple. The ornamental pieces on the roof were covered in gold. I asked my translator why some of that money wasn't spent on those living in abject poverty. He told me that the priests believe that the poor should not be helped as it's their fault that they are poor. If poor people take the little they have and give it to the temple priests, they might be reincarnated in a better situation next time. They call it karma. No mercy, no grace, no hope.

When I was in seminary in London, I used to visit All Soul's Church and listen to John Stott teach. This is how he described grace: "Grace is love that cares and stoops and rescues." Grace is the opposite of karma. We get what we don't deserve: the love, mercy, forgiveness of God. Grace is unmerited favor. Grace is here for you right now, in the middle of what is hard or not working. The writer to the Hebrews described it this way: "Let us then with confidence draw near to the throne of grace, that we may receive mercy and find grace to help in time of need" (Heb. 4:16 ESV).

God says His grace is enough for you, but the text goes on: "for My strength is made perfect in weakness" (2 Cor. 12:9 NKJV). It doesn't say, "If you're a little short of your own strength some days, Paul, I can make up the difference." No. It makes it clear that we are never supposed to be strong on our own. It's only when we acknowledge our weakness that God's strength shines through and it is perfect.

This brings me back to something I said earlier, which might have sounded harsh.

The bottom line is that we were never designed to be enough. Life is hard, and we all face problems. Those who say they don't have any problems are doing one of these things:

1. Hiding their problems
2. Pretending they don't have any

When we live under the pressure of feeling we have to be enough but are disappointed with where we are, I believe we actually have three choices:

1. We stay in hiding. That's a very hopeless place to rest. It leads to feelings of despair, believing that nothing will ever get better. Despair can lead to depression or anger. It makes us close off from relationships and withdraw. Have you ever been there? I know I have. Perhaps you're in a relationship right now that's not working, and you don't know what to do. You've tried to make changes and the other person doesn't respond, so you get frustrated and angry. Maybe you're in a job you don't like and you see no way out. You feel trapped.

2. We pretend we don't have a problem. I find the level of denial in the body of Christ deeply troubling. The church should be the best place on earth to show up as you really are and tell the truth, but so often it's the opposite. We smile and say we're fine as we drag our weary hearts and unbearable burdens through the church doors, and all too often we leave the same way. Why do we pretend to be okay? Perhaps it's because we are ashamed of what's true. We don't want people to think less of us. We're

afraid they'll reject us. We think we're supposed to be okay because everyone else seems to be okay. I did it for years. When you host a live Christian talk show as I did for five years but inside you're barely hanging on by a thread, what do you do? I smiled to cover up my pain even though I was dying inside. You can be well-known but desperately alone. Pretending that we're okay when we're not leads to anxiety and fear. We're afraid someone will see the real us.

I discovered a third way:

3. We have a gut-level, honest, pour-your-heart-out conversation with God.

I held it together until I couldn't anymore. I remember a night in my bedroom where I literally soaked the floor with my tears. I was bone-tired from pretending to have it all together, from trying to be okay. So, I let God have it. I told Him I was afraid and angry and tired and sad and lonely and confused and everything else I could think of. I didn't edit myself. I just let it all out.

I believe my final words were, "I can't do this anymore."

Rather than feeling rejected by my broken outburst, I felt as if God bent down and said, "I know. I've been waiting."

The First Step in Moving Forward

Tell God the whole truth. It doesn't matter what it is—pour it all out. It may be an affair, an addiction, an abortion. It may be that you are so disappointed, you hate where you are in life. It may be that your husband never pays attention to you or listens. Perhaps your children are a disappointment and you don't know whether to be angry with yourself or with them. Maybe you're divorced and you never signed up for the life you now have to live. Whatever it is,

God knows and invites you to take a walk with Him in the garden and tell Him the whole truth.

> O my people, trust in him at all times.
> Pour out your heart to him,
> for God is our refuge. (Ps. 62:8)

When I began to write this book, I wanted to make it very practical, very hands-on. I've shared my own story in previous books but sometimes wonder if I left my reader with the "What now?" I want to give you more. So at the end of each chapter, I've provided tools, simple steps you might take to move forward. Choose one (or all) that makes sense to you. You may even want to write your own step that feels more authentic—but try not to rush over these. You matter! Starting anything in life is hard. The first step is the toughest. It's a choice, a commitment to change. Even if that first step is a baby step you will be further along than when you began. Ask God to help you. Invite the Holy Spirit to guide you.

Even if that *first step*

is a baby step

you will be

further along

than when

you began.

One Step at a Time

Tell God the Whole Truth

1. Have you ever thought about writing God a letter? You might be surprised by what pours out when you do. Don't edit yourself, just start. Tell God everything. There's something about the practice of writing that engages a different part of your brain. If it helps, read it out loud or read it silently yet in His presence.

2. Find a quiet place to take a walk and meditate on Psalm 61:2:

   > From the ends of the earth I call to you,
   >   I call as my heart grows faint;
   >   lead me to the rock that is higher than I. (NIV)

   Even when David was exhausted, soul weary, he called out to God. I don't know where you are right now. You may have given up on God and yourself, but He has not given up on you. You may be afraid to hope again, but hope begins like a tiny drop of rain. My prayer for you is that as you keep moving forward with the tiniest of steps you will find yourself soaked to the skin.

two

Admit That You Are Stuck and Struggling

For our light and momentary troubles are achieving for us an eternal glory that far outweighs them all. So, we fix our eyes not on what is seen, but on what is unseen, since what is seen is temporary, but what is unseen is eternal.

—2 Corinthians 4:17–18 NIV

When things fall apart, the broken pieces allow all sorts of things to enter, and one of them is the presence of God.

—Shauna Niequist

Traffic is bad in most cities at 5:00 PM, and Dallas is no exception. I was sitting at a red light mentally running through the list of everything I needed to do in the next few days. Christian was a junior in high school and had just hit another growth spurt.

1. New long pants topped the list.
2. I needed to get my nails done since I was teaching at a conference that weekend, which reminded me that . . .
3. I needed to pick up my clothes from the dry cleaners.

I was hoping I had something in the freezer I could rustle up for dinner as I didn't have the energy to face a packed supermarket. As I waited for the light to turn green I looked at the gas gauge and it was creeping toward empty.

I'll deal with that tomorrow, I thought to myself.

Tomorrow's list was getting longer. Finally, traffic began to move. The sun was setting as I turned into our cul-de-sac. I waved to my neighbor, playing with his new puppy on the lawn, pulled into our driveway and then the garage. I turned off the ignition, grabbed my purse from the passenger seat, and headed into the house. Through the kitchen window I could see Barry and Christian playing soccer in the last rays of daylight. It made me smile. Barry didn't grow up playing sports, but he wanted to make sure Christian didn't miss out on anything.

I turned to open the freezer, and, in that moment, it felt as if someone had stabbed me in my lower back. I cried out in pain. Slowly I turned back around and grabbed hold of the kitchen island. I didn't know what had happened. I stood there for a moment catching my breath. Gingerly I took a step forward to see if I could walk, and it didn't hurt; it seemed fine. I decided I must have pinched a nerve for a moment and then it released. I didn't mention it to Barry that night as he is such a worrier. (Christian and I have affectionately dubbed him Eeyore, after the donkey in the Winnie the Pooh tales who expects disaster to strike at every turn.) I was fine for the next few days, and then one morning as I was getting out of the car it felt as if my back locked and I couldn't move. Pain shot down my spine and into my leg. Finally, I lowered myself back down into the driver's seat and waited for the pain to pass. I was afraid to move.

It felt as if I might damage something, so I stayed there until Barry came home so that he could help me out of the car.

Over the next few weeks, the episodes of extreme back pain and difficulty walking were happening more frequently. By this point it wasn't only Barry who was concerned. I knew I needed to see my doctor. When he saw my level of pain and how my ability to walk was being compromised, he referred me to a neurosurgeon. Over the next few weeks I had X-rays and an MRI. Then the doctor ordered a CAT scan with a colored dye injected into my spine. When he had all the results, he called us back into his office. He explained that two of the discs in my lower spine were almost gone and the nerves were being pinched between bone. The pain had now spread from my back down my left leg. I could hardly walk.

"We can try cortisone shots to control the pain and reduce inflammation," he said. "But I'm not sure that'll be enough. You may need surgery."

I decided to start with the shots, as I'd heard some horror stories about back surgeries, so he referred me to a pain management physician. The first cortisone shot didn't relieve the pain at all; he tried it one more time, but it did nothing. I was getting weaker and experiencing more pain each day. By now I spent most days in bed. I felt like a very old woman, like someone who had lost her life. The clinical depression that had seemed manageable in the past now threatened to swallow me whole. There had been so many wonderful opportunities on the horizon just a few months ago. I had a full schedule of speaking engagements coming up and a door had been opened for me in television, but now it felt as if every door had been slammed in my face and I was alone, outside in the hallway.

Have you ever been there? The circumstances are different for every person, but the feelings are similar. It might be that you believed a relationship you were in was growing and leading to a new place in life. If it was a romantic relationship it felt as if a beautiful door had been opened to your future, and now you saw everything through that door. All your hopes and dreams lay on the other side and then suddenly, with no warning, the door was slammed in your face. I watched that happen to a friend of mine. It was heartbreaking. For her, every negative thing, every unkind word that had ever been spoken to her had been canceled out by the sparkling ring on her left hand. It served as proof to her that she was worth loving. When the engagement was broken off it not only shattered her plans, it shattered her heart and her vision of herself. She seemed to wither like a flower no longer in water. She was alone, outside in the hallway.

Perhaps you've longed to be a mom. You've watched as your friends have welcomed not only one but two or three children into their families. You celebrate with them, but a little piece of you is aching inside. You've done everything you know to do. You've put yourself through every punishing and expensive procedure in the hope of becoming a mom, but every time the door is slammed in your face. I received a letter from a woman who didn't give me her name or an address but gave me a glimpse into her life. She had tried for years to become pregnant, and eventually she and her husband saved up enough money to try in vitro fertilization. I can only imagine her joy when she discovered that she was pregnant, but it was quickly decimated. She carried the baby for eight weeks and then miscarried. What a particularly cruel door to be slammed in your face.

In her letter she asked this question:

"How can a God of love allow this to happen?"

I could almost hear the lonely, desperate wail that rose up from the paper and I wept for her. The door that had so brutally shut left her alone, outside in the hallway.

There are so many things that happen in life that feel like the slamming of a door.

The end of a friendship you cherished.

The loss of a job.

A divorce you never saw coming.

A child cutting you out of their life.

A devastating health issue.

The circumstances are different for each person, but the feelings of being rejected, isolated, or heartbroken are crushing. What makes many of these situations much harder to bear is that you had no choice, no say in the matter. I've wondered if the woman who lost her baby didn't give me a name or address because she felt ashamed at asking her question.

"How can a God of love allow this to happen?"

She should not be ashamed of the question or the anger and pain behind it. Her question matters. How could you lose a child and not cry out, "Why?" How *can* a God of love allow such things to happen? When we're afraid to ask those kinds of questions, to rail at God, we're left alone in our pain. I think that's one of the hardest things about those door-slamming experiences; you feel alone. If you have loved ones around you, they can sympathize, but they can't enter in to the depth of the devastation. Life moves on for them but not for you. You are stuck in the hallway. If you don't have anyone close to you, the night is even darker. I've often wondered if some of the epidemic levels of depression and anxiety in our culture stem not simply from a lack of chemicals in the brain but from a lack of connection in our lives. Social media has made us believe we're not alone. We can look at the number of "followers" we have, but *following* doesn't amount to connection. In turn, we can follow a lot of people—famous people we would never meet in our normal lives—and feel as if we have a connection with them, but it's an illusion. If we met them in the street they would pass us by. Having a smartphone in the hallway doesn't meet our real human flesh-and-blood needs.

Think about your life for a moment. Can you identify any door-slamming moments? They may be in the past and you've moved on, but what did you do with the feelings that often accompany them? In my life, I discovered that burying feelings didn't make them go away; rather, it led to anger, fear, and depression. I thought I'd moved on, but I was carrying the baggage from those unexpressed raw emotions with me. It might feel more "Christian" not to bring our anger, pain, or disappointment to God, but I believe it's actually the antithesis of a real relationship with Christ. We become a little less authentic with every experience we bury. Think about it. If you've asked God to intervene in a situation, be it for healing or restoration of a relationship, and nothing changes so you simply stuff your feelings, don't you think it would impact your faith? How would you pray the next time? Would you pray with the same intensity and passion or would you lower the bar of what you believe God can or wants to do? I think the church is full of disappointed Christians who don't know how to admit it. So, what's the alternative? Where do we take that pain, those questions when life feels brutal and unfair? How do we pour our hearts out to God when we feel as if He is the one who has let us down?

When I feel let down, I turn to the Word of God. I don't know what place, if any, God's Word occupies in your life, but in my life it is water and air; it's my lifeblood. When I feel alone and adrift, I open the pages to find myself again. The Bible is not a Pinterest app of happy thoughts and motivational quotes; it is full of the honest, heartbroken cries of those who loved God but felt the painful slam of a door in their face.

The prophet Jeremiah was tired of waiting for God to show up:

> Why then does my suffering continue?
>   Why is my wound so incurable?
> Your help seems as uncertain as a seasonal brook,
>   like a spring that has gone dry. (Jer. 15:18)

His cry is clear. *Enough, God! I am worn out. When are You going to show up?*

Job cursed the day he was born:

> Let the day of my birth be erased,
>   and the night I was conceived.
> Let that day be turned to darkness.
>   Let it be lost even to God on high,
>   and let no light shine on it. (Job 3:3–4)

If you know any of Job's story, you'll remember he lost everything. He was the wealthiest man alive at the time, and all his wealth was wiped out in a day. Then he lost his children. They'd been together in his eldest son's house when a tornado hit the home and not one of them survived. Then Job lost his health, covered in boils from head to toe. It was too much for anyone to bear. He wished he'd never been born.

In the book of Ruth we meet Naomi, who lost her husband and her two sons. When she returned to her home in Bethlehem she was a broken woman. She was in desperate pain and blamed God for it. As she approached her old home, her friends saw her coming and ran out to welcome her. But she stopped them dead in their tracks:

> "Don't call me Naomi," she responded. "Instead, call me Mara, for the Almighty has made life very bitter for me. I went away full, but the LORD has brought me home empty. Why call me Naomi when the LORD has caused me to suffer and the Almighty has sent such tragedy upon me?" (Ruth 1:20–21)

God's Word is full of the honest, desperate, unedited cries of men and women through the centuries who have felt the harsh slam of a door in their faces. They asked the questions we would all ask if we felt we could be honest. Why is it so hard for us to be our authentic, raw selves with God? I believe that one of the underlying issues we struggle with as Christians is reconciling two basic fundamental beliefs:

1. God is love.
2. God is powerful.

The first is a message woven through the entire Bible—not just that God is loving, but that He is the very essence and source of love. The second: God is powerful, almighty. There are countless stories of God's intervention, of His power over everything and everyone. So, God loves us and is able to prevent tragedy from striking our lives. Holding those two beliefs as basic to our faith, it's reasonable to ask, why would an almighty and loving God allow heartbreak to touch us? He clearly is powerful enough to stop bad things from happening, and because He is love, would He not want to? I would love to say that I have an answer for you here, but I don't. As Paul wrote to the church in Corinth, "For now we see in a mirror dimly, but then face to face" (1 Cor. 13:12 ESV).

There are things that happen every day that make no sense at all. That is when I choose, by faith, to remember these things:

1. We are living in plan B.
2. Christ is the Redeemer in plan B.
3. We're not home yet, and Christ has gone to prepare a place for us.
4. Even when the hallway is dark, we are never alone.

The Lord is near to the brokenhearted and saves the crushed in spirit. (Ps. 34:18 ESV)

It may feel as if I've rushed to that place, but I haven't. It's been a long hard road, but as Shauna Niequist observed in the opening quote of this chapter, "When things fall apart, the broken pieces allow all sorts of things to enter, and one of them is the presence of God."[1]

Let me finish my story. In the days and weeks that followed the failure of the final cortisone shot, I spent a lot of time in honest conversation with God. I poured out my heart and my questions.

What if I lose the ability to walk?

What if I won't ever be pain free again?

What if my life that used to look like a wide-open door to the future is now contained in the small walls of my home?

As I brought each very real fear to my heavenly Father, the answer was the same:

I'll be there.

I'll be there.

I'll be there.

As I poured out my fears, I felt held. I felt no judgment, just overwhelming compassion. Sitting with the possibility of a drastic change in how I'd lived up until that point, I saw how I had defined the quality of my life by what I was able to accomplish. I'd placed so much value on *what I do* rather than on *who I am*. God's love for me had nothing to do with whether I ever stood on another stage or wrote another book or traveled another mile. I also saw how at times my understanding of God's love for me was based on how things were unfolding in my life. When things were going well, I felt that God loved me. When things were hard, I felt alone. The unfolding showed me He is always near.

Coming face-to-face with the truth that my life might never again be what I wanted shook my faith to the core, but it was a good shaking. It shook loose things that were cultural beliefs, not scriptural truths. It shook the belief that I had surrendered everything to Christ when I still felt so entitled to the life I wanted for myself. It shook the belief that I was living by faith when I was actually living by

When things were going well,
I felt that God *loved* me.

When things were hard,
I felt *alone*.

The unfolding showed me
He is *always near*.

what made sense to me. I also discovered that God meets us in the shaking when we look for Him there.

I remembered the great promise that the boy shepherd, David, wrote:

> Even though I walk through the valley of the shadow
> of death,
> I will fear no evil,
> for you are with me;
> your rod and your staff,
> they comfort me. (Ps. 23:4 ESV)

There is nowhere on this earth that you and I find ourselves where we are separated from the love and companionship of Christ. The writer to the Hebrews put it this way:

For God has said,

> "I will never fail you.
> I will never abandon you." (Heb. 13:5)

I made a beautiful discovery. God not only lives in the wide-open spaces of our lives, God lives in the hallway, and His presence can be most keenly felt when the door has been slammed in our face. So many of the distractions that had filled my life had numbed me to the whole point of my life: to bring glory to God, to know Him, to allow the Holy Spirit to invade every space. I began to worship in the hallway.

It was time for me to be open to whatever the next season in life might hold, so I made a follow-up appointment to see the neurosurgeon. He made it clear that he could do the surgery, but it would be complicated: "I'll have to go through your back to remove one disc and through the front to be able to get the other. It'll give you some interesting scars and your bikini days might be over!"

I reassured him that since I was raised as a Scottish Baptist that was not a concern. A surgery date was set.

It was still dark when Barry and I arrived at the hospital that morning. I checked in and was taken back to a cubicle where I changed into a gown and had an IV put in my right hand. Barry was right beside me, but let me tell you this: Christ's presence was so palpable it was as if I could take His hand. Not only that, there was a peace about the outcome. I wish I could sit down face-to-face with you right now as I write that. It's easy to write faith statements when you emerge from a dark tunnel, but I want you to know I had His peace in the *not knowing*. Christ offers peace in the not-knowing seasons.

The surgeon came in and introduced me to a second surgeon.

"She'll hold your organs while I go through the front of your body."

It's hard to know what to say to that.

Thank you?

Try to put them back where you found them?

The primary surgeon told Barry that the procedure would be about six hours and he'd let Barry know when it was over. As they wheeled me into surgery my last conscious thought was, as the surgery door closed, *I surrender all.*

I remember coming to in recovery and Barry asking if I could wiggle my toes? I thought it was a such a silly question from a grown man until I remembered where I was. So, I wiggled. Within a few days I could tell that the surgery had been a success and I could walk without pain.

The outcome for you might have been different. As you read this you might be in the most challenging days of your life. When you can't see an end to a situation, it's hard not to give in to despair. Again, I look to the apostle Paul:

> For our light and momentary troubles are achieving for us an eternal glory that far outweighs them all. So we fix our eyes not on what is seen, but on what is unseen, since what is seen is temporary, but what is unseen is eternal. (2 Cor. 4:17–18 NIV)

If you're not familiar with that letter or Paul's life it's easy to dismiss his words. When he writes about *light and momentary troubles* he can seem out of touch with your world. As you look at what you're facing right now, *light* or *momentary* are probably not the words you would chose. But we need to read on. Paul has so much to share with us. First of all, he lets us in on just how extreme his suffering has been so that we don't discount his words, but then he gives us two gifts that will help us when we find ourselves in the hallway. First, his credentials in suffering:

Five different times the Jewish leaders gave me thirty-nine lashes. Three times I was beaten with rods. Once I was stoned. Three times I was shipwrecked. Once I spent a whole night and a day adrift at sea. I have traveled on many long journeys. I have faced danger from rivers and from robbers. I have faced danger from my own people, the Jews, as well as from the Gentiles. I have faced danger in the cities, in the deserts, and on the seas. And I have faced danger from men who claim to be believers but are not. I have worked hard and long, enduring many sleepless nights. I have been hungry and thirsty and have often gone without food. I have shivered in the cold, without enough clothing to keep me warm. (2 Cor. 11:24–27)

I can't imagine that level of suffering. And yet Paul suffered even more. You can read about Paul's stoning in Acts 14.

Stoning was never intended to be a punishment; it was always intended as a death sentence. It's a particularly barbaric way to die, still practiced in some areas of the world. Men are buried up to their waists, women to their chests. To prolong the suffering, no one is permitted to throw a large stone. Everyone who is offended by the condemned one had to be able to take part in the execution and throw their own stone. It's a slow death. So, when they stoned Paul, they assumed they had killed him.

They stoned Paul and dragged him out of town, thinking he was dead. (Acts 14:19)

The list of Paul's sufferings is overwhelming, so why does he call it "light and momentary"? I believe he does for two reasons. For one, we look around us. For the second, we look up.

The first reason is that nothing you walk through is wasted with God. He redeems every drop of our suffering.

I can't comfort a woman who's lost a child, but if you have lost one, you can. She'll listen to you because you understand.

I can't comfort a woman whose husband walked out, leaving her financially stressed with children to raise, but if you have experienced that, you can.

I can't comfort a woman who longs to be a mom and can't conceive, but if you have been there, you can.

You may not be able to comfort someone who lost a loved one to suicide, but I can.

You might struggle to understand severe depression and mental illness and not know what to say, but I do understand and can offer help.

This is the beauty of brokenness. When we face our losses in the hallway with God and offer the broken pieces to Him, it's amazing what He will do to bind up the broken pieces in someone else's life. This is how our brave brother Paul described it:

> God is our merciful Father and the source of all comfort. He comforts us in all our troubles so that we can comfort others. When they are troubled, we will be able to give them the same comfort God has given us. (2 Cor. 1:3b–4)

The second gift Paul gives us in this letter is to remind us who we are and where we're going.

> That is why we never give up. Though our bodies are dying, our spirits are being renewed every day. For our present troubles are small and won't last very long. Yet they produce for us a glory that vastly

outweighs them and will last forever! So we don't look at the troubles we can see now; rather, we fix our gaze on things that cannot be seen. For the things we see now will soon be gone, but the things we cannot see will last forever. (4:16–18)

He reminds us that although life can be very painful, pain and loss have a shelf life, suffering and struggle have an expiration date. They will not last forever. I imagine Paul sitting with you right now in the hallway, saying, "Come on. Hold on. Look up. Remember whose you are, and this won't last forever."

More than that, Christ is with you in the hallway. He is with you in the operating room. He is with you wherever you are. Right now, you are not alone. Taking the next step can be as simple as this: Acknowledge your struggle to God. Tell Him how it felt to hear the slamming of the door. Let Him know that you are lonely and hurt. Let Him sit with you in the hallway and hear Him say,

I'm here.
I'm here.
I'm here.

God never rushes us through our pain. He sits with us for as long as it takes. But as you begin to receive His comfort, you might look around and see that you're not alone in the hallway. There's someone else there, and they can't even lift their head. They might not listen to me, but they just might listen to you. Perhaps you'd be willing to join me in a prayer I pray every single day:

Lord, give me eyes to see what I might miss. Give me ears to hear beyond what someone might be saying to what's happening in their heart.

Jesus is the Redeemer in the hallway.

Taking the *next step* can be as simple as this: *Acknowledge* your struggle to God.

One Step at a Time

Nothing You Walk Through Is Wasted

1. Consider starting a journal of all you've walked through. Chart your journey, positive and negative. What were some of the hardest things you've ever faced? What are some of the things you are facing right now?

2. Find a quiet place and ask the Holy Spirit to help you remember things you may have buried. If your pain came from abuse in your childhood, it may be wise to walk through this part of your journey with a Christian counselor.

   When Christian was a little boy his dad gave him a child's craft project that included bits of smooth glass and stone. My son didn't think anything beautiful could be made with broken things until they began to lay them out in cement in a heart mold. The finished piece is beautiful. It's one of my most treasured possessions. Have you ever considered doing something like that? Find a craft store and look for a project that is hands-on, making something lovely out of broken things. One of my core beliefs is that it's amazing what God will do with a broken life if you give Him all the pieces.

3. If you're struggling to identify areas where you felt alone, ask God for help with this. Begin by meditating on this promise:

   > If any of you lacks wisdom, you should ask God, who gives generously to all without finding fault, and it will be given to you. (James 1:5 NIV)

three

Change the Way You Think

Don't copy the behavior and customs of this world, but let God transform you into a new person by changing the way you think. Then you will learn to know God's will for you, which is good and pleasing and perfect.

—Romans 12:2

I can say, "I need to love my kids more," but that isn't going to work. You can't fight your way into a feeling. You must change the way you think about your kids, about your husband, about your wife, and that will change the way you feel, which will then change the way you act.[1]

—Pastor Rick Warren

I've never been good at small talk, which is one of the reasons I don't like parties. At parties you're expected to mingle. Mingling is a terrifying concept to a Scottish person. We tend to be a little reserved, so making polite conversation with a stranger, while you're stuck in a corner with chicken-on-a-stick, is enough to make us break out in hives. For some time though, there was more going on for me than simple cultural reticence. I lacked confidence in who I was in a crowd of new people. That might sound strange if you consider that I spend a lot of time on stage or on television, but those are roles I'm comfortable in. I know what's expected of me. When I'm on the platform I know I'm doing what God designed me to do. When I'm on television I love the intimacy of looking right into the camera, reminding the one who is watching that just as they are, they are loved by God. (It might sound strange to call a medium like television intimate, but that's how it feels to me.) But on occasions when I found myself in a group of strangers or those I didn't know very well, I felt at a bit of a loss. I would have these ridiculously inappropriate thoughts going through my mind.

Should I stand on the dining table and sing, "The hills are alive with the sound of music?"

Should I pretend I'm praying?

If I walk out backward will they think I'm coming in?

It's probably why I've always been comfortable around dogs. You can get down on the floor with them, scratch their ears, and they're happy. It's all they expect, and they'll wag their tail to prove it. Now don't get me wrong, I wasn't a recluse. I was comfortable around close friends, but in certain circumstances, I struggled. I struggled because of how I saw myself, how I thought about myself. My self-image and negative thoughts impacted how I lived for years. It affected the places I went and the places I avoided.

In 2012 I was invited to speak at a conference in Wembly Arena in London. The conference was being presented by Hillsong Church, a large worldwide church whose main campus is in Sydney, Australia. I was familiar with the amazing worship music they have produced over the years, but I'd never met their senior pastors, Brian and Bobbie Houston. My only connection to Hillsong was through my friend Christine Caine.

The speakers with me that year at "Colour" (the name of Hillsong's conference for women) were Christine, Priscilla Shirer, and Bobbie

Houston. I had traveled from Dallas to London by myself, but once I arrived Bobbie and her team made me feel very welcome and loved. Wembly seats over 12,000 people, which can be a pretty intimidating sight from the stage, but it brought me to tears. I never imagined seeing crowds like that in England. Before I came to America I worked with British Youth for Christ as an evangelist. In those days we struggled to get more than a couple of hundred people to any event, so to see thousands of women worshiping God together was beautiful.

I loved every minute of the conference, but on the last night my insecurities surfaced. We were invited for an after-conference party at the home of an English couple. It wasn't just the speakers who were invited that night but the worship team and several of Bobbie's friends and leaders who had flown in from Hillsong churches around Europe. As everyone gathered backstage and began to pile into cars, chatting excitedly in their cute party clothes, I excused myself—muttering something about a headache—and went back to my hotel. I remember sitting on the bed feeling lonely and a bit lost, but the thought of being thrust into a gathering of people who all looked to be about 5 feet 10 and size 2 was too much for me. I didn't feel trendy enough or witty enough. I'd already worn everything I brought and didn't have pretty party clothes, so I voted myself "off the island."

Even as I think about this now, I know that no one at the party would have cared what I was wearing or whether I was too tired to talk and rolled around on the floor with the dog, the cat, or the hamster. It wasn't about them—it was about me. It was about how *I* saw myself. It was about the way I thought about myself. Ironically, I had shared messages that weekend about being loved just as you are. I even began my first message with a Scripture I had recently discovered. It's perfect for those days when your hair won't behave:

> Your eyes are doves
> behind your veil.
> Your hair is like a flock of goats. (Song of Sol. 4:1 ESV)

I could talk to others about being loved just as they are and encourage them to show up even if their hair looked like stuffing come out of a mattress, but I couldn't seem to grab hold of that message for myself.

Old thought patterns are hard to change. Even though by then I lived in a nice house and had a loving husband and son, the imprint of being the poor kid with hand-me-down clothes, living in government housing, was an identity that was hard to shake. The circumstances of my childhood created a thought process that told me certain things about myself. My father committed suicide when I was five years old, and although I don't believe I ever consciously thought this, I lived believing that I wasn't worth sticking around for. He'd suffered a brain injury before his death, and the last time he ever looked at me it was with anger and what I read as hate. So, I lived a careful life. I was careful not to get too close to anyone so that if they walked away it wouldn't hurt so much. When I went into high school I never tried to be friends with the popular girls because I knew they wouldn't accept me. Instead I volunteered for projects or auditioned for a part in the school musical. I was always much more comfortable with something to do because I had little confidence in who I was.

You would think when I became a Christian all of that would have changed, but it didn't. I believed God loved me because He's God. This may sound a little disrespectful, but I thought, *Well, that's His job*. It's not personal. He loves everyone. It didn't change how I saw myself or how I believed others saw me. As a young girl I found my value in what I *did* for God. I volunteered for everything at church and stayed late to clear things up after youth group. Once I became a singer (my first ten years in ministry I was a contemporary Christian artist . . . ask your mother!) and then a television host and Bible teacher, I believed I had value because God was using me, so therefore He must be pleased with me. I didn't understand that God wanted to totally transform the way I thought and therefore how I lived. Not only that, I didn't understand that the greatest, most profoundly personal love story ever is the one between God, in Christ, and any man or woman who will come with nothing and accept His everything. That would take me many years along a broken road to begin to understand.

The way I thought about my worth spilled over into my relationships with other women. I felt they accepted me for what I did and who they perceived me to be. By the time my son, Christian, was in school I had already written several books and been on television, so the other mothers knew who I was. I just didn't let them get to know who I *really* was.

I hadn't allowed the love of God to bathe my eyes a second time. Do you remember that story from Mark's Gospel?

> When they arrived at Bethsaida, some people brought a blind man to Jesus, and they begged him to touch the man and heal him. Jesus took the blind man by the hand and led him out of the village. Then, spitting on the man's eyes, he laid his hands on him and asked, "Can you see anything now?"
>
> The man looked around. "Yes," he said, "I see people, but I can't see them very clearly. They look like trees walking around."
>
> Then Jesus placed his hands on the man's eyes again, and his eyes were opened. His sight was completely restored, and he could see everything clearly. (8:22–25)

While he was healed of physical blindness, at times we need to be healed of spiritual blindness. We're invited to come back to Christ over and over again to be renewed. Having our vision clarified is a powerful gift, an ability to see ourselves as Christ does, not by the labels we wear or the way we think about ourselves. It's not that He's unaware of everything that makes you you and me me. He knows all our little quirks and personality traits, but the glorious truth of the gospel is that Jesus is in love with us right *now*, even though we are a crazy, mixed-up bunch. He sees us as beautiful.

He knows all our little quirks and personality traits, but the *glorious truth* of the gospel is that Jesus is in love with us right now, even though we are a crazy, mixed-up bunch. He sees us as *beautiful*.

I don't know if or where you struggle most in your mind. It may not be with how you see yourself. It may be how you see yourself in other ways, like a parent. You look at all the other parents and how well their children behave in church and you see them roll their eyes when yours raise their voices but not in worship. You question yourself mercilessly.

What am I doing wrong?

Why won't they listen to me?

Why are my sister's children doing well in school and mine are failing miserably?

We judge ourselves so harshly as parents and at times read that judgment into the eyes of others even when it's not there.

One of the most difficult things to bear is when one of your children turns away from faith. That is heartbreaking, and the thoughts that circulate inside are torturing. You wonder what went wrong. Your son went to the same church, the same Sunday school as your friends' son who's grown into such a godly young man, and your boy wants nothing to do with Jesus. What happened? What did you miss?

One of my dearest friends is there right now. We have wept together over the phone as she's shared what's going on in her child's life. She is a great mom. She is loving and fair, strong and tender but at the moment she can't see herself that way. Her grief has blurred her vision. She looks at the situation that is not okay and in her mind that translates as *she's* not okay. That's a huge, important distinction.

One of my main passions as a mom from the moment my son was born was to help him distinguish between doing a bad thing and being a bad person. He was an easy child to raise, but when he was sixteen he did something foolish and fortunately got caught. It wasn't a huge deal, but it was out of character for him. He's such a perfectionist and mentally beats himself up if he falls short of his tough internal standard. Later that night he saw me praying for him and crying in my bedroom. He came rushing in with tears running down his face, saying that he'd never do anything bad again. I gathered him in my arms and assured him that I was quite sure he would! I told him that night what I wish I'd understood at sixteen or even at thirty-six: what he did wasn't a good thing, but that didn't make him a bad person. It made him human. I told him that God loves him as much on the days he feels he's done everything wrong as He does on the days he feels he's done everything right. I told him that life will take some unexpected turns, and at times he'll be devastated, but never to doubt for a moment that God is in control. I told him to stop trying so hard to be perfect and just live, loved.

He looked at me and said, "May I ask you a question?" I said, "Of course," wondering what profound question my little speech had stirred. He said, "If you're okay now, can I go back to watching television?" Yes . . . profound!

Perhaps you don't question yourself as a mom; that might be the one thing you know God gifted you to be. You may wrestle with how you see yourself as a wife. You look at how affectionate your friend's husband is with her and how distracted or uninterested your husband is and wonder what you're doing wrong. You look back to the days when you first fell in love, when he loved everything you did and laughed at every funny thing you said. How could things have changed so much? You look in the mirror, and with blurred vision you think the problem is you. You've tried to talk to him, even suggested counseling, but he's not interested. In your mind, there's something wrong with you.

Or, perhaps you are the one who has lost interest. You wonder how you'll ever find your way back to the way you felt on your wedding day. You can't imagine that you used to think it was cute when he dropped his socks right beside the laundry basket instead of in it or left his plates in the sink when it's only two more steps to the dishwasher. Now everything he does annoys you. Not only that, the passion is gone. When you think about your marriage you feel angry and sad. You believe you'll never be happy again unless you can get out.

I'm a huge fan of the Hallmark Channel at Christmas. I love every snowy movie and every love story even though I know exactly how each one is going to end. I wonder, however, how those romantic tales impact our lives. A steady diet of happy endings, though fictional, can blur our vision. It's not only darkness that changes what we see. Rose-colored glasses can too. Those kinds of movies don't show the hard work that goes into a marriage when it would be much easier to throw in the towel. They don't depict the seasons when the only thing that holds you together is the commitment you made to God and to each other, not how you feel when you look across the dinner table. Changing the way you think can impact the most important relationships in life.

I went through two years when I struggled in my marriage. I was disappointed and hurt and angry. I allowed myself to move into a way of thinking where everything he did was wrong. I discovered too in that season that it was easy to find women who encouraged me to walk away. I had to choose carefully who I listened to. It was my commitment to God and to our son that held my feet to the fire. Today, I look at Barry as he tells me to stay inside because it's cold and he'll take the dogs for a walk, or listen to him talking to our son on the phone, and I love him more now than I did on our wedding day. I did not believe that was possible, but it is.

Even as I write that, I think of those of you whose marriages didn't survive, and I pray that my words don't condemn you, because that's not my heart at all. You may have fought for your marriage and it failed anyway. You may have had an affair and your husband wouldn't forgive you, or you may simply have wanted out and got out. The breathtaking truth of the gospel of Jesus Christ is that we are not judged on our failures but on the finished work of Christ. Clearly that doesn't mean we get to live any way we like, it simply means that there is always an open door back to the Father when we fall down. That is the heart and passion of this book. It's okay not to be okay, because Jesus has made us right with God. If we could

It's okay not to be *okay*,

because Jesus has made us

right with God.

begin to grasp that, it would radically revolutionize our lives. God looks down on this crazy, mixed-up bunch of beautiful that is the body of Christ and He loves us. He doesn't love the one who fought for her marriage one bit more than the one who gave up. You're not an outsider, not second best. If you have placed your trust in Christ, you are a child of God.

> See what kind of love the Father has given to us, that we should be called children of God; and so we are. (1 John 3:1 ESV)

As I've reflected on some ways we need to transform our thinking, it's clear that we live in a culture that places value on things that are external—looks, wealth, position, and success. You may not be married or have children, but do you wrestle with your basic value as a person? If you didn't get the promotion you expected or if you weren't invited to join a certain group heading out for lunch, it's very easy to feel undervalued or insignificant, and that can begin to change how you think about your life. I received an anonymous letter a few weeks ago from a woman who told me she struggles to connect with anyone. She goes to church but sits at the back and slips out during the final piece of music. She didn't tell me why she feels so unlovable, but the last sentence of her letter was this: "I think if I disappeared tonight no one would notice that I'd gone." That is a wretched place to be. We were made for connection and long to know that we matter.

I've talked to many women whose greatest mental struggle is that they don't believe they measure up as a Christian. A young girl told me she's sure God must be disappointed in her because she doesn't pray enough or have enough faith. Another woman told me she believed God isn't answering her prayers because He doesn't love her as much as He loves some of the other women in her church. Instead of feeling deeply loved, many feel overwhelmingly condemned. I don't believe this is how God wants us to live. There has to be a transformation in our thinking.

Change Your Mind

In the first two chapters we looked at having a gut-level honest conversation with ourselves and with God, facing the disappointment when doors have been slammed in our face. But none of that will move us forward unless we change how we think. How do we change what we think when it's so deeply entrenched?

Let's take another look at the beginning of Romans 12. The English Standard Version translates verse 2 this way:

> Do not be conformed to this world, but be transformed by the renewal of your mind, that by testing you may discern what is the will of God, what is good and acceptable and perfect.

Paul makes it clear that the only way to be transformed is to have our minds renewed. As I've meditated on this verse for some time, I wonder if in contemporary Christianity we place more emphasis on behavior than on right thinking, on what we do rather than understanding why we do it and committing wholeheartedly to the process.

Let me explain what I mean. One of the things that our son noticed in his first year of college was that some of the other students he'd known at high school or church changed the way they behaved when they were away from home. Now, I know a certain amount of that is to be expected when our children are first away from home. This, however, was more than a simple spreading of wings. They lived like completely different people. Once they were away from parents watching their behavior, they behaved however they wanted. If there's not a transformation internally, then when external forces are removed, we do whatever pleases us. I've prayed with so many Christian parents who are devastated by the way their college-age kids have changed. *"They never behaved like that before they left home!"*

The hard question remains: Why did they live differently at home? Did they make good choices previously to fit in, to avoid discipline, or because there was a heart and mind change? You can do all the right things, but if you don't know why you're doing them you'll abandon them when they're no longer expected. It's not just our children. It's very easy for us to fall into the same trap. In our culture we are increasingly bombarded with messages about what to wear, what to think, who to believe, what the latest trend is. Paul's words to the church in Rome speak clearly to us today: *Don't copy the behavior and customs of this world.*

It's the most natural thing in the world to copy behavior and customs or Paul wouldn't have begun that way. We all want to belong, to fit in. When we give our lives to Christ, it becomes clear that some behaviors and customs are no longer in line with the Word of God. So, we may stop doing certain things, but unless we are transformed, unless our minds are renewed, not much has really changed internally. Some of us simply replace the world's list with a more acceptable one. We swap drunkenness for gluttony or cursing for gossip. Until we understand that we may live on this earth but we belong to another kingdom, we'll tidy ourselves up a bit and wonder why we still feel so defeated. Giving our lives to Christ is not like joining a club. It's a call to a radical new way of thinking and living 24/7—not just on Sunday mornings and when we're at church.

The word *transformed* only occurs one time in all four Gospels, and it was a dramatic transformation:

Six days later Jesus took Peter and the two brothers, James and John, and led them up a high mountain to be alone. As the men watched, Jesus' appearance was transformed so that his face shone like the sun, and his clothes became as white as light. (Matt. 17:1–2)

The word for *transformed* here is the Greek word *metamorphoo*. From that root we get our word *metamorphosis*. When a beautiful butterfly emerges from a cocoon, the change is total. As the disciples watched that day, Christ's face shone like the sun, His clothes white as light. I can't imagine what that must have been like to see, but do you know that one day you and I will look like that? Christ told His disciples that when He has finally defeated Satan and established a new kingdom and a new earth, "then the righteous will shine like the sun in their Father's Kingdom" (Matt. 13:43).

A day is coming when our transformation will be complete. We will be changed externally and internally. But now, as followers of Christ on this earth, we are called to be transformed internally, which will impact our external behavior. Only an internal transformation will truly change external behavior. Every battle begins in our minds, not with our behavior. We can behave a certain way and remain unchanged. If we want to change how we act, we have to change how we think.

You may be tempted to ask, "Why did you call this book *It's Okay Not to Be Okay* if now you're telling me I have to change?" Good question! The answer is simple. It's not an issue of judgment, it's a matter of freedom. Christ wants you to be free. Free from condemning thoughts, free from compulsive behaviors, free to be who you really are, free to live your crazy, beautiful life.

When Paul wrote to the church in Galatia he said,

> So Christ has truly set us free. Now make sure that you stay free, and don't get tied up again in slavery to the law. (Gal. 5:1)

Paul wanted to make sure the believers in Galatia didn't fall back into condemnation under the law. They were being told by someone they had to be circumcised to be right with God. Paul reminded them there is only one way to be right with God and that is through faith in Christ and His sacrifice on the cross, once and for all, for those who trust in Him.

You may have been touched by that kind of message in more contemporary ways. Some churches place great emphasis on a particular style of dress or music. Some believers drink wine and some don't.

Only an internal *transformation* will truly change external behavior. Every battle begins in our *minds*, not with our behavior. We can behave a certain way and remain unchanged. If we want to change how we act, we have to change how we *think*.

Some churches invite women into the pulpit and others don't. Some of it is custom and some a particular understanding of a certain passage of Scripture. That's fine. But if anyone ever tells you that you're not saved unless you follow their rules, run as fast as you can, because that is not the gospel of Jesus Christ.

So, how do we live in the freedom that Christ paid for? We lean into that wisdom from Romans 12—we pursue renewal through the transforming of our minds.

You might be tempted to ask, "What's wrong with my mind?" You're smart, well educated, and computer savvy, with endless information at your fingertips—quite different than the audience Paul wrote to. The problem is not a lack of information; it's a lack of renewal. We live in a fallen world, which means our minds are fallen too. We were made to worship, but unless our minds have been renewed, we don't worship God, we worship what *we* want. The question remains, How do you renew your mind? The word *renewal* found in Romans 12:2 occurs only one other place in the Greek New Testament, and it gives me great hope that this process is not something you and I can do by ourselves. We can't. We need the Holy Spirit.

> But when the kindness and love of God our Savior appeared, he saved us, not because of righteous things we had done, but because of his mercy. He saved us through the washing of rebirth and renewal by the Holy Spirit. (Titus 3:4–5 NIV)

Renewing our minds is a beautiful joint work between our commitment to become more like Christ and the transforming power of the Holy Spirit working in us. What do I mean by that? What's our part? Someone asked me one day what I'm most committed to. I had a few answers: Christ, my family, helping other women find freedom, working to help victims of sex trafficking, . . . my dogs. He then said, "Look at where you spend most of your time and that will tell you what matters to you." I thought about that for a while. Some seasons of life are more demanding than others. If you have young children, not much of your time is your own. But if you're like me, we find time for what we think we need to relax. You might love to bury your face in a good book with the bathroom door closed! Or if you have an allegiance to a particular television show, you'll make time for it. I've had to ask myself, Does what I'm doing with my spare time refresh me or am I simply zoning out? Now, don't get me wrong: I think at times zoning out is just what we need, but it doesn't work toward the renewing of our mind. That's where the choices we make determine whether we're working with the Holy Spirit or not. Just as we have a Savior who loves us, we have an enemy who hates us. He will do all he can to distract and condemn.

When I began to realize how much of my life was still being influenced by destructive thought patterns, I made some changes. They were not monumental leaps, they were simple steps, one day at a time. I saw that I had an internal problem (my thoughts) and an external problem (the things I allow to impact me). I made my internal and external problems a matter of intentional prayer. Let's face it: no matter how hard we try to change, it's hard. So,

1. I began, daily, to ask the Holy Spirit to change my heart. I asked Him to soften my heart and teach me true humility.
2. Then I began to work with Him. I eliminated programs I watched or magazines I read that fed into a wrong way of thinking. I spent time with friends who brought me closer to Christ. I prayed, prayed, prayed. I talked to God about everything. I read good books by godly men and women, but more than that, I made the Bible my best friend. I discovered that when I began to work with the Holy Spirit, rather than thinking, *I have to do this if I want to be more like Jesus*, I found myself wanting to do the things that brought me closer to Him and brought glory to the Father. That's when you begin to see

that your mind is being renewed: when the things you think you should do become the things you simply love to do.

So, where do you begin to take the next step?

Start where you are. Don't think, *I have to read the whole Bible in the next six months.* Begin with prayer. Ask the Holy Spirit to soften your heart and to open your eyes. Find a translation of the Bible that you can understand. I read the New Living Translation for devotional reading, but if I'm studying a passage I love the English Standard Version and the New International Version.

Talk to God. He loves you so much. Don't think you have to use fancy words. He's your papa, just talk.

Then give yourself a big hug. We're not perfect but we are redeemed, so give yourself a break. The truth is, I'm a bit weird and a little eccentric, and it's taken me quite some time to see that (a) Yes, I am . . . and (b) that's okay!

One Step at a Time

Choose to Walk Past Your Past

1. Pay attention this week to how you spend most of your time. You may be a busy mom and don't really have any time for yourself. You may be in a job that leaves you drained and exhausted, but when you finally flop down in your favorite chair, what then? Our lives are so busy, but when you have those moments to breathe, how do you use them? Do you turn on the TV and let its messages wash over you? Don't get me wrong, I have my favorite shows like you do, but I have also carved out time each day to pay attention to what I'm thinking. You are a work in process and deserve time invested in who you are becoming. Think of your life as a painting: what are the brush strokes you're adding each day? Take back some time. Even if it's five or ten minutes, find a quiet place, away from the noise, and listen to the tapes that play in your head. Write those down even if they're very negative. This is not about passing a test; it's about being honest with yourself about where you are and then taking a step forward.

2. Capture your thoughts. Be aware of the familiar negative thoughts that invade your mind and grab hold of them as quickly as you can. Paul writes this to the church in Corinth:

> We demolish arguments and every pretension that sets itself up against the knowledge of God, and we take captive every thought to make it obedient to Christ. (2 Cor. 10:5 NIV)

Take every thought captive. Grab hold of every negative thing you've ever believed about yourself and replace it with truth. This step will not be easy. It'll take work. You may have believed lies about yourself for years, but Christ wants you to be free. Here are a few of the truths I remind myself of when I find myself in a negative thinking pattern:

I am a child of God.
I am loved.
I have a future.
God is for me.

Find the truths that speak loudest to you and begin to change the way you think.

four

Face the What-Ifs Even If You Are Afraid

Cowardly Lion: "All right, I'll go in there for Dorothy. Wicked Witch or no Wicked Witch, guards or no guards, I'll tear them apart. I may not come out alive, but I'm going in there. There's only one thing I want you fellows to do."
Tin Man and Scarecrow: "What's that?"
Cowardly Lion: "Talk me out of it!"

—*The Wizard of Oz*

For God has not given us a spirit of fear and timidity, but of power, love, and self-discipline.

—2 Timothy 1:7

God hasn't given us a spirit of fear, but it's something that many of us struggle with every day. It can work for us or against us. It can paralyze us or serve to warn of impending danger.

I've watched how it plays out with animals in the wild. A few years ago I spent some time in Kenya visiting and taking supplies to children who had been sponsored through the relief agency World Vision. At the end of our trip, our local hosts offered to take us on an all-day safari on the Maasai Mara, Kenya's largest game reserve. I was excited at the prospect of seeing animals in their natural environment. We set off at dawn, binoculars, sunscreen, and water bottles in hand. Our driver told us he couldn't guarantee which animals we would see, but he would do his best. We drove for some time over rough roads in an open jeep, and then, as we turned a corner, we saw zebras, so close we could almost touch them. Stunning. Black-and-white stripes as if they'd been freshly painted that morning. They looked at us as if we were the weird-looking ones and ran off. Then giraffes. So elegant with beautiful markings and gentle faces. We drove for another couple of hours without seeing anything, and then suddenly our driver stopped the jeep and pointed off in the distance. I grabbed my binoculars and looked. It was a group of very large hippopotami knee-deep in mud at the edge of the Mara River. I immediately started to sing that famous hippo song from my childhood at full volume:

> Mud, mud, glorious mud
> Nothing quite like it for cooling the blood . . .

The driver turned around and respectfully asked me to be quiet, which I tried not to take personally.

"Can we get a little closer?" I asked.

"Not if you want to see another day!" he said. "The hippo is one of the most dangerous animals in Africa."

Enough said!

The sun was beginning to set, and it was time to turn back to the Keekorok Lodge where we were staying that night. As we crested a hill I spotted an impala. It had become separated from the pack somehow, and instead of running with the long, graceful strides I expected, it was standing perfectly still as if frozen. I asked our driver

Face the What-Ifs Even If You Are Afraid

why it wasn't moving. He pointed off in the distance, to a clearing in the trees. There he was: a magnificent lion stalking his prey. He told us that the impala is much faster than the lion, but they can become literally frozen in fear. I wanted to yell and tell it to run, but the driver told me to be quiet . . . again!

Fear can serve to protect us, but it can also paralyze us and keep us from being who we were created to be. That's part of my story. The first time I was invited to speak and teach, I said no. It was a fabulous opportunity with a conference that God was clearly using to touch women's lives, but I was terrified. I was comfortable as a television host or as a singer, but the thought of standing up with a microphone in front of a group of women was horrifying. There were so many thoughts racing through my mind:

What if I can't remember my message?
What if I freeze on stage?
What if I say something that doesn't make sense?
What if I need to use the restroom?
What if I'm terrible?

The host of the event persisted. I said no again the second time, but the third time, they asked me to pray about it. What a low blow! I presented the same what-ifs to the Lord. The overwhelming sense was simply, *Just be present. You don't have to be perfect.*

Now before you think I have some hotline to heaven where I hear the audible voice of God, I don't. But after years of walking in relationship with Him, reading my Bible, and listening to the quiet promptings of the Holy Spirit, I know His voice in my spirit. So I said yes to the invitation.

I'd love to tell you that once I said yes I was overwhelmed with a sense of peace. I was not. I was still terrified, but I showed up. I'd also love to tell you that once I walked out onto that platform and looked out at the crowd of eight thousand women I became the greatest preacher since Charles Spurgeon. Again, I did not. Halfway through my message I saw that my image was being displayed on gigantic screens around the arena and I started to laugh. Then I saw that my hair was sticking up at the back so I tried to fix it. We all had quite a giggle that day, but I'm not sure my message stayed with anyone. Now, twenty-five years after that first speaking engagement, I have a whole new understanding about what you and I are called to do. We're called to show up! It'll never be about us getting anything perfect, but when we are present God can do what only He can do.

You may think this doesn't apply to you since you may not be a speaker, but it affects every area of life. After my father's death my mum had three children to raise alone. We were seven, five, and two. She had very little income but a rock-solid faith that God had promised to be a husband to the widow and a father to the fatherless. After my father's death she asked God for two things:

1. She asked that we would all come to faith in Christ at an early age.
2. She asked that she would live to see us all grown and settled in our careers and calling.

God honored those prayers. Each of us made commitments to Christ before we were ten years old. On to prayer number two. My sister was the first to graduate college, and she became an elementary school teacher. I was next and after graduating from seminary began working with Youth for Christ. Finally, after seven years of study, my brother graduated as an architect.

I flew home to Scotland to spend a little time with Mum after Stephen's graduation. Sitting by the fire one morning, cups of tea in hand, I asked her, "What now, Mum?" She asked me what I meant. I told her that God had answered those two prayers she prayed when we were all little, so what did she want to pray for now? She smiled that lopsided smile she always had and said she had no idea.

My mum didn't have an easy life. She had to leave school at fifteen to help her mum care for her father who had Alzheimer's. She was only thirty-three years old when my dad died, and she never remarried. I knew there had to have been dreams she'd abandoned when life asked her to step into roles she never imagined for herself. So, I asked her about those.

"What would you have loved to do if circumstances had been different?"

"I'd have loved to be a teacher," she said. "Or lead a Bible study."

I told her that it wasn't too late. "If you still have a pulse, Mum, and there's no white chalk mark around your body, it's not too late. You can start a Bible study in your home."

She looked at me with skepticism, a look I've become affectionately accustomed to in life.

"Why not?" I asked.

Then, understandably, the what-ifs began.

What if no one comes?

What if they ask a question and I don't know the answer?

What if I give a wrong answer?

I don't think any of my neighbors are Christians; what if they're offended?

What if they expect me to pray out loud?

I assured her that I would stay until she'd had the first one, and if she didn't have an answer to a question she could just say, "Sorry, I don't know, but we can find out together." Finally, she agreed to take the first step. We put together a simple invitation, and I dropped them into all her neighbors' mailboxes. (Actually, before my sister reads this and reminds me that we don't have mailboxes in Scotland, I dropped them through their letter boxes. My family is big on accuracy.)

The night arrived, and Mum was very nervous. We set out a few extra chairs in her lounge, not sure who, if any, would come. Five women came. Mum asked if I would open in prayer.

"God, thank You for tonight. Thank You for these ladies who've come. We'd love to learn more about You. Amen."

It was an amazing evening. Mum and I had gone to our local Christian bookstore and bought several copies of a simple study on John's Gospel. We began with lesson one but didn't get very far.

"Who is 'the Word'?"

"What does it mean that He existed in the beginning with God? Was He God's brother?"

"The light shines in the darkness . . . is he talking about the moon?"

It was so great to sit with a small group of honest women who understood very little about God or the Bible or faith and weren't afraid to ask questions. (Less than 2 percent of the population in Scotland go to church.) Mum did a great job. In her quiet, kind way she answered as many of the questions as we had time for. I stayed quiet, praying for her every moment. At the end, I served them tea and scones and listened as they chatted about life and the weather and their aches and pains. That night, my mum's lounge became a holy place. Nothing was perfect, but we were all present and God was with us. Several weeks later I wept with Mum on the phone as she told me that one of her neighbors had given her life to Christ as the message of the Gospel of John became real to her.

I wonder what the what-ifs are in your life? Fear and the questions that give it fuel hold us back from stepping out in faith and living the life we long for. I think we're afraid we'll get it wrong, be misunderstood or rejected, or fail. The reality is, all of those things are possible, but they don't have to stop us. When I was a young girl, a friend brought me a necklace from her trip to Israel. It was a little glass ball, and inside was a tiny mustard seed. This Scripture verse was inside the box:

> Jesus told them. "I tell you the truth, if you had faith even as small as a mustard seed, you could say to this mountain, 'Move from here to there,' and it would move. Nothing would be impossible." (Matt. 17:20)

I spent the next twenty years concentrating on how hard it would be to move a mountain and forgot all about the size of the seed. The seed was tiny, one of the smallest seeds there is. The people who listened to Jesus that day thought of mountains as pillars that held up the sky. In his commentary on the Gospel of Matthew, R. V. G. Tasker writes this:

> To move a mountain was a proverbial expression for overcoming a great difficulty. The meaning of this verse is that strong faith can accomplish the apparently impossible, for the man of faith is drawing upon divine resources.[1]

It is God that moves the mountain, we just need the tiny seed of faith. If even that feels overwhelming, here is what theologian R. T. France writes:

> It is important to observe here that it is not the "amount" of faith which brings the impossible within reach, but the power of God, which is available to even the "smallest" faith.[2]

I love that. God takes us where we are, and when we step out and offer Him the smallest wisp of faith, He moves on our behalf. But if we sit around waiting for the fear to disappear, we'll probably be sitting for a while.

Do It Afraid

I had the privilege some years ago of interviewing Elisabeth Elliot, widow of Jim Elliot. If you're unfamiliar with their story, here's a little background: Jim and four of his missionary friends had a passion to witness to an unreached people group, the Auca Indians of Ecuador, with the gospel of Christ. They knew that the Auca were a dangerous tribe with a reputation for mass killings and believed the only way to stop that was if they came to faith in Christ. Using their Mission Aviation Fellowship plane, they had spent some time lowering supplies to the tribe during various flyovers and felt it was finally time to meet face-to-face. One morning in 1956, each of the five men from their group was lowered onto the beach. They waited to see what might happen, but nothing could have prepared them for what they saw next. A group of Auca warriors emerged from the trees with their spears raised, ready to throw. Jim had a gun in his pocket, but even as he reached for it he knew he couldn't use it. These five men had promised they would never kill an Auca who didn't know Christ just to save themselves. All five men died that day.

One of the beliefs Jim lived by could not have been more beautifully potent than on that dark morning:

> He is no fool who gives what he cannot keep, to keep what he cannot lose.[3]

When Jim was killed, Elisabeth was left to raise their ten-month-old daughter, Valerie, by herself in a foreign country. Can you imagine the what-ifs that must have gone through her mind?

What if the men hadn't gone there that day?
What if they'd spent more time lowering gifts and messages?
What if he'd waited until our daughter was older?

When I try to put myself in her shoes, I imagine my first thought would be to get my daughter and myself on the first plane out of there. That's not what Elisabeth did. She believed that God had sent them there as a family and the job wasn't finished. She told me, however, that her life was completely controlled by fear. Every time she wanted to step out in faith, fear stopped her. The what-ifs were overwhelming. Then a friend told her something that changed her life. Her friend said, "Why don't you do it afraid?"

Together with Rachel Saint, the sister of Nate Saint (one of the murdered missionaries), they went on to finish the job their loved ones died for—reaching the Indian tribes of Ecuador, including the very people who had murdered their loved ones. When her daughter was just three years old, Elisabeth and Valerie moved in and lived with the tribe for two years, seeing many come to faith in Christ. The name Auca was a disparaging name given to the tribe by other tribes. It means "naked savages." Their real name is Waodani, which means "true people." Each one of the warriors who had killed the missionaries came to faith in Christ and became His true people.

That is clearly a very extreme story. Few of us will be called to make that kind of sacrifice. But Elisabeth, who died a few years ago, has helped us with a step along our path.

Do it afraid.

The what-ifs that so often hold us back usually have their roots in a flawed belief system. We believe that if we're going to take a step out, we have to be sure that whatever we're attempting will be successful. I don't think that's what we're asked to do. I believe we're asked to step out in faith and leave the results to God. Perhaps you've stepped out in the past, convinced that God had called and equipped you, and things didn't turn out as you expected. That can feel devastating. You may have had a broken relationship with a family member, and after praying over the situation you knew that it was time to make the first move, but it went terribly wrong. That's confusing. Or you were sure that God told you it was time to ask for a raise at work, knowing it was long overdue. Confident, you went to your boss and presented your case. You did it respectfully and convincingly, but it wasn't received that way. Instead of moving forward it felt like you took two steps back. Those types of experiences can shut us down inside. They can make us angry with ourselves, angry with the one who didn't respond well, or even angry with God.

When You Step Out and God Doesn't Step Up

The prophet Elijah knows how you feel. You might ask, "What can a prophet who lived thousands of years ago in a different world and culture have to say that will help me right now?" Let me say, a lot! I've known the bare bones of this story since I was a child, but when you begin to put flesh onto those bones there is much for us to learn. A little background information on what was happening in Israel at the time will give us context. Ahab and Jezebel were king and queen of Israel. Rather than being faithful to God, they introduced the worship of Baal, a cult of sex, wealth, and power. The writer of 1 Kings writes this about Ahab:

> He did more to provoke the anger of the Lord than any of the other kings before him. (16:33)

God spoke to His prophet Elijah and told him it was time to confront this blatant idolatry. Now we come to the part of the story you may be familiar with, the knockout fight on top of Mount Carmel. Elijah invited all the prophets of Baal, some four hundred and fifty of them, to join him and King Ahab on the mountaintop to determine once and for all who is the true God. He set out the ground rules. Each side would take a bull, slaughter it, cut it into pieces, and put it on top of an altar. Then, introducing no fire, they would call on the one they serve to consume the sacrifice. Elijah invited the four hundred and fifty prophets of Baal to go first. For hours they cried out to Baal, cutting themselves with knives and swords, which was part of their usual barbaric worship practices, but nothing happened. Elijah began to laugh at them, suggesting they might want to shout louder in case Baal was taking a nap. Then it was Elijah's turn.

> Then Elijah called to the people, "Come over here!" They all crowded around him as he repaired the altar of the LORD that had been torn down. He took twelve stones, one to represent each of the tribes of Israel, and he used the stones to rebuild the altar in the name of the LORD. Then he dug a trench around the altar large enough to hold about three gallons. He piled wood on the altar, cut the bull into pieces, and laid the pieces on the wood.
>
> Then he said, "Fill four large jars with water, and pour the water over the offering and the wood."
>
> After they had done this, he said, "Do the same thing again!" And when they were finished, he said, "Now do it a third time!" So they did as he said, and the water ran around the altar and even filled the trench.
>
> At the usual time for offering the evening sacrifice, Elijah the prophet walked up to the altar and prayed, "O LORD, God of Abraham, Isaac, and Jacob, prove today that you are God in Israel and that I am your servant. Prove that I have done all this at your command. O LORD, answer me! Answer me so these people will know that you, O LORD, are God and that you have brought them back to yourself."
>
> Immediately the fire of the LORD flashed down from heaven and burned up the young bull, the wood, the stones, and the dust. It even licked up all the water in the trench! And when all the people saw it, they fell face down on the ground and cried out, "The LORD—he is God! Yes, the LORD is God!" (18:30–39)

Can you imagine what that must have been like? Elijah had placed his trust in God and God had showed up in ways that must have astonished even him. He'd asked for them to wet the wood to make it harder to burn, but God burned up not only the bull and the wood,

He consumed the very stones, the water, the dust. No wonder the people fell on their faces.

Elijah ordered every one of the prophets of Baal to be executed. From Elijah's perspective, the evil in the land had now been purged. He was confident that Ahab and Jezebel would repent and all of Israel would return to worshiping the one true God. So, given special strength from God, Elijah ran all the way to Jezreel where Ahab and Jezebel had their palace. The only reason he would have gone there was that he was sure of the outcome. As he waited to be called into the palace and thanked for helping turn a nation back to the one true God, he received a message from the palace—but not the one he expected.

> Jezebel sent this message to Elijah: "May the gods strike me and even kill me if by this time tomorrow I have not killed you just as you killed them." (19:2)

Elijah couldn't believe what he was hearing. He'd done everything God told him to do. He'd put his life on the line as one man against four hundred and fifty, and now the queen had taken a sacred vow upon her own life that by the same time tomorrow, Elijah would be dead. So he ran. I'm sure he was worn out from the contest, but more than that he didn't understand what was happening. Why hadn't the king and queen repented at such a clear show of power? What was the point if no one changed? He went as far as Beersheba, about a hundred miles, with his servant, and then he let him go. It's as if he was saying, "I'm done. You were my servant when I was a prophet, but I quit."

He traveled on by himself into the wilderness and that evening collapsed in exhaustion under a tree. Before he fell asleep he prayed,

> "I have had enough, LORD," he said. "Take my life, for I am no better than my ancestors who have already died." (19:4)

He was exhausted, confused, and depressed. He'd faced his what-ifs, and the final outcome made no sense.

What if I heard God wrong and He doesn't consume the sacrifice?
What if the prophets of Baal kill me on the mountain?
What if they have some trick and manage to set fire to their
sacrifice?

He'd faced them all and stepped out; God showed up in power, and as far as he could see, nothing had changed. The false prophets were dead, but more would rise up to take their place. Elijah was done.

If you've ever felt discouraged like this, you know it's a devastating place to be; it just doesn't make sense. Perhaps you were part of the start-up of a church plant that you knew God had called you to. You left a home and an area you loved out of simple obedience, and after a great start it suddenly went terribly wrong. Or you invited a friend, a coworker, or a neighbor you've been praying for to an Easter service. The service is amazing, God is clearly in the house, people give their lives to Christ at the end, but the one you brought is more turned off than ever. Perhaps your child who's been disinterested in faith asks for a Bible. You know this is an answer to prayer, but after a few weeks they give it back saying it didn't make any sense. Your worst fears are realized that spiritually they have no hunger for God. There are so many times in life when after we find the courage to face our fears and step over the what-ifs, things don't turn out the way we knew they should.

I promised there would be things from Elijah's story that would help us, but the help is actually not from Elijah's life; the help is all about God. It's about what God does when we've come to the end of ourselves. The next part of the story is such a picture of grace.

But as he was sleeping, an angel touched him and told him, "Get up and eat!" He looked around and there beside his head was some bread baked on hot stones and a jar of water! So he ate and drank and lay down again. (vv. 5–6)

An angel touched him. I find that very moving. There's something so healing about a simple touch. Not only that, he told Elijah to eat and drink. He didn't lecture him or ask why he ran away. He didn't address Elijah's wish to die; he just cooked for him. The word here for *angel* also means "messenger." It's possible Elijah thought this was a passing stranger who took pity on him. There's no "fear not" greeting, and so after eating and drinking, he fell asleep again.

> Then the angel of the LORD came again and touched him and said, "Get up and eat some more, or the journey ahead will be too much for you." (v. 7)

This time the writer identifies the angel as "the angel of the LORD." Warren Wiersbe helps us understand more about who that was:

> In verse 7 the visitor is called the angel of the Lord, an Old Testament title for the second person of the Godhead, Jesus Christ, the Son of God.[4]

Several places in the Old Testament (see Gen. 16:7, Exod. 3:1–4, Judg. 2:1–4) we have appearances recorded of the angel of the Lord. In fact, in Exodus 3:44 the angel is referred to as "God" and "the LORD." This type of appearance is called a *theophany*, which means "appearance of God." How merciful that Christ Himself would touch this worn-out man with no word of judgment, just loving care for the needs of his body. Elijah had quite a road ahead of him. He was heading for Mount Sinai, one of the most holy places in Jewish history, but it was about two hundred miles away. It took Elijah forty days and nights. It should only have taken him about two weeks. I wonder why, when he was running for his life from a crazy woman, he took so long? Perhaps his thoughts were on Moses and the children of Israel who wandered for forty years in the desert. In years to come, Christ would spend forty days and nights in the wilderness as well.

Why was Elijah heading to Mount Sinai when he felt as if his life was over? He went to the very place where God met Moses. He went to the holy mountain. He needed God to meet him there. When I think of that intentionality, I remember the response that Peter gave to Jesus when Christ asked the disciples if they would leave Him too:

Simon Peter replied, "Lord, to whom would we go?" (John 6:68)

Does that resonate with you? It does with me. Even at my lowest point in the deepest pit of depression when I too prayed to God to take my life, the only place I knew to go for help was to Him. Elijah made his way up the mountain and into a cave. Some translations give us *cleft* instead of *cave*. Perhaps this was the very cleft in the rock where Moses waited for God to pass by. Exhausted from his journey, Elijah spent the night in the cave. But then God asked him a question: "What are you doing here, Elijah?" (1 Kings 19:9).

God knew exactly why Elijah was there, just as He knew where Adam and Eve were when He asked them, "Where are you?" (Gen. 3:9). God's questions are never to inform Himself; He knows everything. The questions are to reveal to *us* what's going on inside of us.

Elijah replied, "I have zealously served the LORD God Almighty. But the people of Israel have broken their covenant with you, torn down your altars, and killed every one of your prophets. I am the only one left, and now they are trying to kill me, too." (1 Kings 19:10)

After Elijah poured out everything that made no sense to him and gave God the picture from his perspective, God called him to the entrance of the cave.

And as Elijah stood there, the LORD passed by, and a mighty wind-storm hit the mountain. It was such a terrible blast that the rocks were torn loose, but the LORD was not in the wind. After the wind there was an earthquake, but the LORD was not in the earthquake. And after the earthquake there was a fire, but the LORD was not in the fire. And after the fire there was the sound of a gentle whisper. (vv. 11–12)

Again, after this earth-shaking display God asks the question, "What are you doing here?" Elijah gave the same answer he'd given before.

I've served You faithfully!
I'm the only one who did it right.
I'm the only one left.
There's nobody who stayed faithful but me!
Now they're trying to kill me!

Then the Lord let Elijah in on the bigger plan, the one that had always been in place. He told him to go back the way he came and to anoint Hazael to be king of Aram. Then He told Elijah to anoint Jehu to be king of Israel and anoint Elisha to replace himself as God's prophet. He told Elijah that these three men would take care of everyone who had turned away from worshiping God, but that He would spare 7,000 who had never bowed the knee to Baal. He showed Elijah that he was not the only one left; there was a large crowd of faithful people still serving God no matter how it felt to him.

Have you ever been tempted to discount everyone else because they don't seem as faithful as you? Do you ever question another denomination because they don't do things the way you do? Do you ever get so discouraged by the state of Christianity that you're ready to throw in the towel? God is moving even when we can't see Him. God is in control even when things seem out of control. When the wind and the earthquake and the fire hit the mountain, Elijah was protected by the rock. The rock took the blast just as Christ, the Rock, took the full force of the wrath of God on Himself on the cross so that you and I can lean in to the gentle whisper of God when we don't understand what's going on around and inside us.

The what-ifs will always be there. We're human. And even when we push past them and take a step of faith, things might not always work out in a way that makes sense to us. But this I know for rock-solid sure:

You don't have to be perfect, just present.

You can pour out your what-ifs to the Lord.

When you take that step and things seem to go wrong, God is working, God is faithful, and God is a God of grace.

What are the what-ifs holding you back? Are you willing to take a step and see what God might do? Just know this: when you've come to the end of yourself and you don't get it, take a nap, have a good meal, and lean in for the gentle whisper of God. For every what-if that crosses your mind—and trust me, they still cross mine—allow the truth of God's Word to be louder than the clamor of fear.

> I praise you, for I am fearfully and wonderfully made.
> Wonderful are your works;
>> my soul knows it very well. (Ps. 139:14 ESV)

For nothing will be impossible with God. (Luke 1:37 ESV)

Jesus looked at them intently and said, "Humanly speaking, it is impossible. But with God everything is possible." (Matt. 19:26)

God is *moving*

even when we

can't see Him.

God is in *control*

even when things

seem out of control.

One Step at a Time

Don't Quit—Every Step Counts

1. Remind yourself that this is not a quick fix. Facing the what-ifs will be a challenge, even when you've started to make progress, because it's so easy and tempting to quit. We're on a journey, not a day trip.

2. Don't let fear take control. Write down everything you're afraid of. Fear is a huge obstacle that can paralyze us. Remind yourself of this promise every time fear begins to grab hold of your heart: "For God has not given us a spirit of fear, but of power and of love and of a sound mind" (2 Tim. 1:7 NKJV).

   This is thought to be the last letter Paul ever wrote. He was in prison and facing execution. Many believers had abandoned him because it was now, under Emperor Nero's rule, a crime to be a Christian. Half of Rome had been burned to the ground. For many, the what-ifs had happened. Here Paul shows us that even in the darkest night we don't have to be afraid because God is in control.

3. What if you have given up? Tell God that you've given up, it was too hard, you've quit. Then ask Him to help you start again. Take the list of everything you're afraid of and read it to Him. Change the place fear holds in your life.

   F . . . fall on your face before Him.

   E . . . earnestly seek Him.

   A . . . ask Him to give you His peace.

   R . . . rest in His presence.

five

Let Go of What You Can't Control

I have learned to kiss the waves that throw me up against the Rock of Ages.

—Charles Haddon Spurgeon

And we know that God causes everything to work together for the good of those who love God and are called according to his purpose for them.

—Romans 8:28

I had no idea how much I would be faced with the issue of control until I became a mother. Our son didn't walk until he was fourteen months old. By then friends and family expressed concern that he was behind the appropriate markers for his age and size. I told them I was convinced my son, who could crawl at the speed of a Lexus, had no interest in markers and would walk when he was jolly well ready to. And he did!

I was speaking at an event in a large arena, and Barry brought Christian to the edge of the stage to crawl to me. He'd been doing that for weeks. It was his party trick. That night, however, he paused for a moment, looked around at the crowd, at me, and then he got up and walked. I remember thinking, *I do hope he doesn't require an audience for all major milestones in life. This could be challenging.* But Christian simply liked doing things at his own pace. It was the same with potty training. I introduced the concept of moving from diapers to big-boy pants with the enthusiasm one usually reserves for a trip to Disney World. According to all the child-rearing textbooks he was at the optimum age. But he was not impressed. He said, *No, but thank you.* Then one day I took Christian and one of his friends, who was a few months older, to McDonald's for lunch. After their Happy Meals and running around in the playground for a while, his buddy announced that he needed to use the bathroom. Christian made the significant discovery that day that his friend was wearing Toy Story big-boy pants. It was a eureka moment. On the drive home he announced, "Mom, I'm done with diapers." He never wore them again.

One of the greatest lessons parenting makes clear is that we are not in control. With children, we're not in control of the moment they decide to be born, how they'll feed, what they're willing to eat or spit up. We're not in control of how they sleep, or don't. Christian was not a fan of sleep for the first nine months, at night or for naps. I thought I might lose what little of my mind I had left. We absorbed every piece of advice from friends who swore that they had found the one thing that would make the most reluctant baby sleep like an angel. We tried them all. We sat his car seat on the clothes dryer. We ran the vacuum cleaner in his bedroom until there was no pile left on the carpet. We sat him by the bath and let the water run until we were concerned we might be solely responsible for the apparent water crisis in our state. Barry put his car seat in the car and drove him around until he fell asleep, but the moment he brought him inside, he resumed the angst-filled cry of the midnight warrior. One evening Barry, seeing how exhausted I was, told me that he'd be on duty all night so that I could finally get a full night's rest. At about 2 AM I heard Christian begin to cry, but Barry got up straight away. I pulled the covers over my head and tried to go back to sleep but I couldn't. It seemed unnaturally quiet in the other room, so I slipped out of bed to check on them. It was quite a sight to behold. Barry was fast asleep on the sofa with Christian in his arms. On closer examination Barry was holding the bottle in Christian's ear. Minimal nutritional value there. But it worked!

The word *control* is, in itself, neither positive or negative. Its weight and meaning rest in what it's attached to. In many situations control is very important. When you're walking in a busy crowd with a child you need to be in control. If you struggle with food, alcohol, or any addiction, control is your friend. Scripture encourages us to have self-control.

> A person without self-control
>   is like a city with broken-down walls. (Prov. 25:28)

> But the Holy Spirit produces this kind of fruit in our lives: love, joy, peace, patience, kindness, goodness, faithfulness, gentleness, and self-control. (Gal. 5:22–23)

There are, however, many situations where the word *control* has negative weight. When we call someone a "control freak" it's clearly not a compliment. Spouses often complain about a controlling wife or husband. In the workplace no one wants a controlling boss or coworker. People have sometimes left their church home because the leadership is too controlling.

Reflecting on my own life, I know that experiencing a negative event in childhood can heighten the need for control later in life. If you've experienced sexual, physical, verbal, spiritual, or emotional abuse as a child, the feeling of being out of control is crushing. Many women and men struggle with eating disorders later in life to try to cope with abuse from childhood, as if to say, "This is one area I get to control." In those situations, if you dig a little deeper, underneath that need to control lies one of the greatest enemies of our souls: shame. Life is scary to one who lives with shame, and what feels like the antidote, *control*, is actually its own prison. I know because I lived that way for many years. I had no control over my father's anger and ultimate suicide. The confusion, fear, grief, and shame that produced in me pushed me into a desperate need to control something. I didn't turn to food or alcohol—mine was darker and more twisted. I tried to control the love of God. For years I lived under the burden of trying to be good enough for God, but because it looked good on the outside I was never challenged by anyone. If you show up drunk at your Bible study, people will notice. If your weight has skyrocketed, it shows up in the real world. But if you're the one who volunteers for everything at your church, who leads a Bible study, who speaks, who sits on national television every day and talks about the love of God, only He knows whether you're serving out of pain or passion, out of a genuine calling or a devastating wound.

I believed it was *not okay **not** to be okay*, so I relentlessly pushed myself to fix myself. Did I know I was addicted to that pursuit? No. I thought I was living a life that was pleasing to God because I worked so hard to be worth loving. That worked until it didn't anymore. I believe the mercy of God allows us at some point in life to hit the wall and, when everything else falls apart, we are held by His mercy. Sometimes we reach that place at the bottom of a bottle or in the wrong person's arms. Sometimes we reach it when we realize that we are resentful of the people who don't notice how much we're doing for them and for God. I reached it on the floor of my room in a psych hospital. However we get there, it's devastating. Everything that has made sense until that point in life is now exposed as a sham. For me, that agonizing, lonely place where I, like Elijah, asked God to take my life became the place where I heard that still, small voice, that whisper: *I love you. Always have. Always will. Rest for a while. Let go.*

The true, unadulterated gospel of Jesus Christ is that God loves us so much that He sent Jesus Christ to take our place on the cross. When Christ cried out, "It is finished," He was saying, "The bill is paid in full." He took the shame, the punishment on Himself so that when we are in relationship with Him, when we trust that finished work on the cross, we are forgiven, we are loved, and we are free. There is nothing that you or I can add to what Jesus has already done.

I love the song "God Is in Control." It was an immediate radio hit because the lyrics were so encouraging. They spoke to the truth of God being in control no matter how things appeared and declared our response that we would not be shaken.

Those are powerful lyrics, but what do you do when the circumstances of your life don't match the lyrics? Where do you go when life feels out of control and God appears to be oblivious to your pain? What do you do when, as far as you can see, you have been forsaken? Who do you turn to when you're shaken to your very core? What do you do when you're absolutely convinced that you heard God's plan for your life, but nothing is falling into place?

These are some of the most foundational questions we can ask in our lives. These questions matter, and God never shies from things that matter to our souls. If, right now, you find yourself in a place where life feels out of control and nothing seems okay, my heart leans toward you, but more than that, God's Word speaks directly to you in that lonely, confusing place.

God Is in Control

In my life, the greatest truth that helps me let go of what I can't control is the foundational belief that no matter how things appear,

God is still on the throne. I don't think any story in the Bible unpacks what that looks like more than the story of Joseph in the book of Genesis. I write *what it looks like* because often our idea of God being in control is radically different than this story. We want to believe that if God is in control, things will fall into place. If that doesn't happen we want to understand why, and we want to know in a timely manner. That's not Joseph's story.

In Acts 7 we read the heartbreaking story of the stoning of Stephen. He was a young man full of the Holy Spirit, an ardent follower of Christ. Some of the Jewish religious leaders wanted to get rid of him, so they persuaded a few men to lie about him, saying that he had blasphemed the name of God. Stephen was dragged into court where the High Priest asked him if the accusations were true. Instead of attempting to defend himself from their lies, he gave a stirring account of the history of the Jewish people and the faithfulness of God from generation to generation. When he came to Joseph's story, he said this:

> Jacob became the father of the twelve patriarchs of the Israelite nation.
>
> These patriarchs were jealous of their brother Joseph, and they sold him to be a slave in Egypt. But God was with him and rescued him from all his troubles. And God gave him favor before Pharaoh, king of Egypt. God also gave Joseph unusual wisdom, so that Pharaoh appointed him governor over all of Egypt and put him in charge of the palace. (vv. 8b–10)

"But God was with him and rescued him from all his troubles."

Twelve words, a capsule of the truth. But when we step back into Joseph's story we see it took thirteen years for those twelve words to unfold. Thirteen years is a very long time to believe that God is with you when every circumstance of your life says otherwise. Joseph's story begins in Genesis 37 and takes us right to the closing of that book. The final words recorded in Genesis are these:

"Soon I will die," Joseph told his brothers, "but God will surely come to help you and lead you out of this land of Egypt. He will bring you back to the land he solemnly promised to give to Abraham, to Isaac, and to Jacob."

Then Joseph made the sons of Israel swear an oath, and he said, "When God comes to help you and lead you back, you must take my bones with you." So Joseph died at the age of 110. The Egyptians embalmed him, and his body was placed in a coffin in Egypt. (50:24–26)

Just as Joseph had no idea when God spoke to him in a dream that the promise he'd been given would take years to be fulfilled, his brothers had no idea that God would indeed lead the Israelites back into the Promised Land, but they wouldn't live to see it. It would be a long time in the future, and the people would be led by a man called Moses.

God Intended It for Good

We're introduced to Joseph as a teenager in Genesis 37:

Jacob loved Joseph more than any of his other children because Joseph had been born to him in his old age. So one day Jacob had a special gift made for Joseph—a beautiful robe. But his brothers hated Joseph because their father loved him more than the rest of them. They couldn't say a kind word to him. (vv. 3–4)

Jealousy is a cancer in family relationships, particularly in blended families. In those days—and now if you watch the TLC network— men had more than one wife. Jacob had four wives, so his children had different mothers. That's hard enough, but then add in that Joseph was the baby of the family and his mother was Jacob's favorite wife, Rachel. A perfect storm on the horizon.

In Sunday school, I was taught that Joseph was given a coat of many colors, but in reality, it was a richly ornate coat. It was foolish of Jacob to show such favoritism toward one son, because it didn't turn them against their father, it turned them against their brother. When parents clearly favor one over another it causes a lot of pain and resentment. When there's a second marriage and children are involved it takes wisdom to know how to navigate those potentially troubling waters. When our son was in elementary school, the principal sent a note home with each child saying that a special school counselor had been hired to help children walk through the heartache of divorce, as so many of the children were acting out in school. I have friends who have blended families, and I've watched them do it beautifully, but it took time, patience, wisdom, and more than a few tears.

Well, Joseph not only received the coat, he wore it around his brothers even though it clearly irritated them. He was just a boy. At seventeen you do what seems good. Medical science tells us that the frontal lobe, the rational part of the brain, is not fully developed until twenty-five.[1]

I wish Jacob or Rachel or one of the other wives had been able to nip Joseph's grandstanding in the bud. If the other sons didn't have a good word to say about him it must have been clear to them all, but they let it go. There is wisdom here for us. Don't ignore the genesis of a problem, because it will only grow. With Joseph, it grew exponentially. God had an amazing plan for Joseph's future, but unlike Mary, the mother of Christ who "kept all these things in her heart" (Luke 2:19), Joseph let them all come right out of his mouth.

One night Joseph had a dream, and when he told his brothers about it, they hated him more than ever. "Listen to this dream," he said. "We were out in the field, tying up bundles of grain. Suddenly my bundle stood up, and your bundles all gathered around and bowed low before mine!"

His brothers responded, "So you think you will be our king, do you? Do you actually think you will reign over us?" And they hated him all the more because of his dreams and the way he talked about them. (Gen. 37:5–8)

At the beginning of the chapter Joseph is with his brothers in the field caring for their father's flocks, but just a few verses later, he's not. Perhaps, as verse 2 makes clear, it's because he enjoyed tattling on them. The text doesn't tell us why some time later Jacob sent Joseph to see his brothers. Perhaps he had regret that there was a breach in their relationship, and he knew that he had contributed to it.

Although we don't know the reason, that decision would prove to be disastrous for Jacob and set him up for years of heartache. When the brothers saw Joseph coming, they decided to get rid of him once and for all: they would kill him. Reuben, the eldest brother, intervened and suggested they throw him into a well and leave him to die. The other brothers agreed to that. So, when Joseph arrived they ripped his fancy coat off his back and tossed him down the shaft of a well. Reuben intended to come back later and rescue Joseph, but it would be too late. The other brothers saw a caravan of camels heading to Egypt, and they sold their baby brother as a slave.

Reuben was devastated when he realized that Joseph was gone. Regret is a punishing emotion. I can't imagine what he felt. How he must have agonized over his choice to go along with part of a plan that was wrong. When we allow ourselves to take one step in the wrong direction, intending later to take two steps back, we don't often get that chance to make another choice. It would be many years before Reuben would get to see that even though he didn't step up and save his brother, God did.

What about Joseph? Try to put yourself in his shoes. He knew that he'd heard from God. He knew that at some point his whole family would bow down and worship him. He didn't know when, but he knew that God had revealed it to him in a dream. Now, he's bloodied and bruised at the bottom of a well. The natural question to ask is, "Can someone else mess up God's plan for my life?"

Have you ever asked that? The circumstances will be different, as few of us will literally end up at the bottom of a well, but the principle stands.

You were engaged to be married. You had waited for the right one, and finally God brought him or her along. Then at the last moment, a former love interest rears their uninvited head and the engagement is broken off. You wonder, *How could this happen? Now my whole life is out of control.*

You knew that God was preparing you to take over the Bible study at your church. You waited patiently, and then at the critical moment when the former teacher stepped down, the church leadership chose someone else. They made a mistake! They chose the wrong person.

You've been married for years. You have children that you're committed to raise in a healthy family, but then your spouse says they want out. You fight it, pray over it, but in the end, you have no control and they leave. Have they messed up God's plan for your life? Are you condemned by someone else's choice to live a second-best life?

You've lived your life with integrity in the workplace or at church, and then someone spreads a rumor about you that's not true. You're sure that no one will believe it because of who you are, because of your character, but they do. You are outraged, and you are alone. Have they just messed up God's plan for your life?

I say a resounding no. Can people harm you? Yes. Can people lie about you and break your heart? Yes. I had a colleague some years ago who told some people I was working with that I was a pathological liar. He told them that I had made up the story of my father's death to get sympathy. He said the whole story was a lie. I couldn't begin to fathom why he would do that, but what was much harder to bear were those who, at first, believed him. I remember lying facedown on my bedroom carpet, sobbing until my eyes were so swollen I could hardly see. Later that night, I opened my Bible to a favorite Psalm and read these words:

> Those who live in the shelter of the Most High
> will find rest in the shadow of the Almighty.
> This I declare about the LORD:
> He alone is my refuge, my place of safety;
> he is my God, and I trust him.
> For he will rescue you from every trap
> and protect you from deadly disease.
> He will cover you with his feathers.
> He will shelter you with his wings.
> His faithful promises are your armor
> and protection. (91:1–4)

There are moments in life when there is nothing you can do to control what's happening. In those times, find your hiding place under the shelter of God's wings. That night I had to let go of what I couldn't control and trust my Father.

As we look further into Joseph's story we'll see several turns in the road that he could not have seen coming, but when he was finally reunited with his brothers, as they bow before him begging for mercy, Joseph said this:

> You intended to harm me, but God intended it all for good. He brought me to this position so I could save the lives of many people. (Gen. 50:20)

Even when people intend to harm us, God is still in control. No matter what their motive was or how it impacts our life for a time, God is with us and He will bring good from it. That's what Paul was saying to the church in Rome when he reminded them that "God causes everything to work together for the good of those who love God and are called according to his purpose for them" (Rom. 8:28). He didn't say that all things were good or that all things feel good. He simply reminded them and us that God had promised to bring good, even from the most painful circumstances of life. It just

There are *moments* in life when there is *nothing* you can do to control what's happening.

In those times, find your

hiding place

under the shelter of God's wings.

doesn't always happen on our schedule. One of my mum's favorite Scriptures was this classic:

> "For I know the plans I have for you," says the LORD. "They are plans for good and not for disaster, to give you a future and a hope." (Jer. 29:11)

It's tempting to pull out an encouraging verse of Scripture and put it on a T-shirt, but when we do that we miss the context, and actually, we miss the greater hope. If you go back just one verse in Jeremiah 29, to verse 10, you read, "This is what the LORD says: 'You will be in Babylon for seventy years. But then I will come and do for you all the good things I have promised, and I will bring you home again.'"

I have yet to see that verse on a T-shirt! Now, before you throw this book at the wall because I've ruined your favorite verse, sit with it for a while. God in His mercy was preparing His people for what was ahead. He gently says to us, *Don't panic that you've been carried away. Don't think everything is out of control. I'm letting you know that this will take some time so that you won't fix your eyes on what you see but on what I have promised.*

Jesus did the same thing. In the last conversation He had with His closest friends, recorded in John's Gospel, He tried to prepare them for the events that were about to unfold. They couldn't understand at the time, but they would be able to look back and remember.

> I have told you these things so that you won't abandon your faith. (16:1)

A Culture of Perception

Our problem is that we view our lives through the window of our culture rather than the rock-solid promises of God's Word. We live in a culture of perception. We perceive certain people to be winners or losers depending on how the circumstances of their lives fall into place.

I got the job and you didn't; I win. I'm in control

He chose me, not you; I win. I'm in control.

He got the promotion and I didn't; I lose. I have no control.

His son made the football team and mine didn't; I lose. I have no control.

When we view our faith through that window, we've corrupted it. We've either reduced God to a vacillating rich uncle who gives one day and takes away the next or someone who doesn't care about us, who allows our lives to be blown around with no plan in place. The truth is that whether we win or lose, we're not in control. We never have been. God is in control and He is for us. When we believe that, only then can we let go of what we don't understand and trust God.

Let's go back to Joseph's story. There's a lot we could unpack, but I want us to focus on what we read at what appears to be the worst moments in his life. Remember when he was sold to a caravan of traveling salesmen on camels? From our point of view, by that time he's been the subject of two experiences that appear to be out of his control: first he's thrown into a well by his brothers, and then he's sold as a slave. But then we read this:

> When Joseph was taken to Egypt by the Ishmaelite traders, he was purchased by Potiphar, an Egyptian officer. Potiphar was captain of the guard for Pharaoh, the king of Egypt.
> The LORD was with Joseph, so he succeeded in everything he did as he served in the home of his Egyptian master. (Gen. 39:1–2)

The Lord was with Joseph. We need to stop right there. That is a profound, eye-washing truth. It's tempting to think, *If the Lord was with Joseph, why did he end up bruised and battered in a foreign country? Why didn't God protect him?* When we look at our own lives we think, *Surely if God is with me terrible things won't happen.*

Can you identify moments like that? When things went wrong, what went through your mind? Did it feel as if God was in control or that He'd taken His eyes off you for a moment and when He looked back was surprised at the chaos? Until we embrace the understanding that God, and no one else, is in control, our faith remains shaky. When we begin, by faith, to grasp hold of this truth as deep as the marrow in our bones, it changes us. We don't have to be afraid anymore. Hymn writer Edward Mote said it so well:

> My hope is built on nothing less
> Than Jesus' blood and righteousness;
> I dare not trust the sweetest frame,
> But wholly lean on Jesus' name.
> On Christ, the solid Rock, I stand;
> All other ground is sinking sand.

Joseph had no control over his new situation, yet he brought everything he had to serve his owner. I'm challenged by that. There are times in life when we're expected to do things that are "not our job." How we respond in those moments tells us a lot about ourselves. Will we serve, or say, "This is not okay. Do you people know who I am?" Our position in life should never determine our posture in service. As Joseph began to settle into life in Egypt, Potiphar, his owner, recognized the hand of the Lord on this young slave and promoted him to head of his entire household. Okay, now the story makes more sense, we think. He had a little bump in the road, it was pretty devastating at the time, but now Joseph's ministry is back on track. God has blessed his obedience and his brothers will be bowing down in no time. Thank you, Jesus! Well, don't break out the sparkling grape juice just yet—there's more.

> Joseph was a very handsome and well-built young man, and Potiphar's wife soon began to look at him lustfully. "Come and sleep with me," she demanded. (Gen. 39:6b–7)

Joseph didn't give in to despair, but will he be tripped up by sexual temptation? How many people in positions of influence have fallen over this obstacle? Sex is a powerful force. It's a beautiful God-given gift when it's expressed inside the commitment of marriage, but when we're tempted to move outside that bond, it causes pain and heartache.

This isn't a temptation only for those in positions of authority, of course. We might read about those people on the news, but the truth is, it's a temptation that impacts us all. I've walked beside a couple of friends who had affairs, and it was devastating for everyone involved. My friends never thought they would be capable of something like that. The truth is, we're all capable of anything. When we allow the temptation to be louder than the prompting of the Holy Spirit, the unthinkable can become reality. What looked enticing in the moment for my friends was full of regret when it was over. We live in a culture and time that has removed God's standards and branded the unthinkable acceptable. Not just acceptable, normal. That's why we have to bury our hearts in the Word of God, which is, as David wrote, "a lamp to guide my feet and a light for my path" (Ps. 119:105).

So how did Joseph respond to sexual temptation?

> But Joseph refused. "Look," he told her, "my master trusts me with everything in his entire household. No one here has more authority than I do. He has held back nothing from me except you, because you are his wife. How could I do such a wicked thing? It would be a great sin against God." (Gen. 39:8–9)

It would be hard to imagine a more honorable response. Joseph refused to break trust with his master, but more than that, he recognized that the one he would ultimately sin against was God. Although he determined to do the right thing, Potiphar's wife would not give up. One day when no one else was around she grabbed

Joseph by his cloak and tried to pull him into her bedroom. He tore himself free from her grip, but she held onto his cloak as he ran from the house. When her husband came home, she accused Joseph of attempting to rape her. Potiphar was furious that the servant he'd given so much authority to had betrayed him, so Joseph was thrown into prison. So unfair. Joseph had done everything right. He'd even shared part of his testimony with her—I can't sin against my God—and yet, he ended up in prison. In that situation it would be tempting to believe God is not in control: *If God is in control how could I end up in prison for doing the right thing?* Once more we read this:

> But the LORD was with Joseph in the prison and showed him his faithful love. (v. 21)

Joseph had no power, no lawyer, no control. There was nothing he could do but keep being the man he was becoming. He let go of what he couldn't control and once more threw himself into service. The young, arrogant teenage boy was turning into a man of real integrity and character. The prison warden was so impressed with Joseph that he put him in charge of all the other prisoners. One of the greatest lessons of Joseph's life is that God is far more interested in who we are becoming than what we are doing. When things went wrong, it didn't turn him away from God. He stayed faithful. It's easy to become bitter or discouraged when things don't go the way we hoped they would, particularly when we've honored God. Joseph continued to serve.

We don't know how long Joseph spent in prison. He was seventeen when he was brought to Egypt and thirty when Pharaoh brought him out of prison and made him his second in command. The dreams he'd had as a boy were about to make sense in God's timing. Joseph had the gift of being able to interpret dreams. Some time into his sentence, Pharaoh's chief cupbearer and baker offended him and landed in prison with Joseph. One morning he noticed that they both looked deeply troubled, so he asked them what was wrong. They told him they'd had dreams the previous night that bothered them. They had no idea what the dreams meant. Joseph assured them that interpretations belong to God, and he invited them to tell him about their dreams, which they did. For one, it was good news. He was about to be restored. For the other, the outcome would not be so good. He was about to be put to death. Then Joseph did something that's worth noting. He asked the man who was about to be restored to do something for him.

> Only remember me, when it is well with you, and please do me the kindness to mention me to Pharaoh, and so get me out of this house. (40:14 ESV)

Everything Joseph said to the two men came true. One man was executed and the other restored, but he forgot his promise to Joseph. Joseph would spend the next two long years in prison. I wonder if Joseph got tired of waiting for God to deliver him? It had been a long, hard road and he'd been faithful, but nothing was happening. God hadn't delivered him. In his humanity, he tried to exercise a little control and turned to the cupbearer for help. If God had forgotten him then surely the cupbearer wouldn't. It's easy to understand. When something drags on for a long time we just want it to be over, so we try to fix it ourselves. It didn't work for Joseph and it didn't work for me. In my spirit I heard God say, *You can run around and try to put out every little fire, or you can fall on Me and when the time is right, I will deliver you.*

Two years later Pharaoh had a dream, and no one could interpret it. Then the cupbearer remembered his promise and told Pharaoh about Joseph. The rest, as they say, is history. Joseph interpreted the dream, and then put a plan in place to prepare the nation of Egypt for an upcoming famine because Pharaoh made him his prime minister. When the famine hit, the nation was saved. But the famine traveled outside of Egypt to Canaan where Joseph's brothers and his father, Jacob, lived. There's a lot of drama in the remaining chapters as the brothers discover that not only is Joseph alive, he's in charge. There is a beautiful reunion between Joseph and his father as the story comes to an end. For us, the gift Joseph gave to his brothers is a gift for us to tuck deep into our hearts: *You intended to harm me, but God intended it all for good.*

Joseph doesn't try to cover up the motives of his brothers; they were clear. They initially left him for dead then sold him as a slave . . . *but God.* Those two words change everything.

You may have been betrayed . . . but God.

You may have been abandoned . . . but God.

You may think that right now, everything is out of control . . . but God.

Can you bring to God whatever feels out of your control and, by faith, say, "I don't understand but I trust You. I choose to let go"?

The first verse I learned as a child was Psalm 46:10: "Be still, and know that I am God."

The Hebrew root that's translated *be still* means "let go." When we *let go*, we acknowledge to Him, "You are God."

One Step at a Time

Don't Panic, God's Got You

1. Write down the areas of your life that you struggle to control. It may be your marriage, your children, your job, your mind, your spending, or your eating. Whatever it is, put it down on paper and face it. Offer each area up to God and ask Him to help you let go.

2. There are many names for God in Scripture. Here are a few. Meditate on these. Find the one that speaks most to your fears.

   Elohim . . . The Strong Creator God.

   Adonai . . . Lord of All.

   El Roi . . . The God Who Sees Me.

   El Shaddai . . . God Almighty.

   Jehovah-Shalom . . . The God of Peace.

   Jehovah-Rapha . . . The God Who Heals.

   Jehovah Raah . . . The LORD is My Shepherd.

   Take one each day and declare it over your life.

six

Rise Above Disappointment

We can rejoice, too, when we run into problems and trials, for we
know that they help us develop endurance. And endurance develops
strength of character, and character strengthens our confident hope
of salvation. And this hope will not lead to disappointment.

—Romans 5:3–5

If dreams die life is a broken-winged bird, that cannot fly.

—Langston Hughes

W hen I think of all the emotions that make up who we
are, disappointment is one of the hardest to handle. So
many things fall under that one word, but they don't
weigh the same. I was disappointed that the Dallas Cowboys didn't
have a better season last year, but that didn't leave a mark on my
heart. (We always have next year!) Some situations, though, devastate
us and leave us breathless. That happened to me, and it changed me
for good. Three months into my pregnancy with Christian my doctor

told me there was something seriously wrong with him. The actual phrase she used was "incompatible with life." Because I would be forty when he was born, she had recommended extra tests outside the normal ones. Once she had all the results on her desk she called us in and gave us that unthinkable diagnosis. She recommended that we terminate the pregnancy immediately. I said no. No. No. So she said, "We'll see how long you can carry him."

The next few weeks and months were a roller coaster of emotions, but the most constantly present ones were heartache and profound disappointment. I was confused as well. Why had God allowed me to get pregnant only to have this little one die on the delivery table? In my Bible I had underlined this verse when I found out that I was going to have a baby: "Even strong young lions sometimes go hungry, but those who trust in the LORD will lack no good thing" (Ps. 34:10).

Now, this "good thing" was going to be taken away. Why? I remember driving to the beach where we used to live in Southern California and talking to my baby. I said, "I don't know if you heard all that, but I just want you to know that I'm going to fight for you. I'm going to fight for every breath that God has ordained you to take."

I cried and prayed and bargained with God. Facing the disappointment of losing the only child I would probably be able to have shook my faith to the core. It's so easy to quote verses when the sun is shining, but when the day turns black as night, it silenced me. I had to wrestle with the very verse I'd chosen to underline . . . *those who trust in the Lord will lack no good thing.* I thought of friends who'd lost children, whose marriages had fallen apart, whose physical health was decimated. This verse had to mean more than I wanted it to mean. What is still standing when everything else is gone? I found the answer on my knees and through my tears.

Christ my Savior. God my Father. The Holy Spirit my Comforter.

The "good thing" I wanted, I might not get. The "good thing" that remained was greater.

A couple of weeks before Christian was born, my doctor called to tell me that the same day my test results had come back, the results of another forty-year-old patient were also returned. My results were accidentally put in her chart, and hers were put in mine. There had never been anything wrong with Christian. Before I could begin to celebrate, I suddenly realized that another woman was getting a very different call. I dropped to my knees and prayed for her. Who was she? Did she know Christ? How would she bear this news? My doctor was not able to tell me her name, but heaven knew her, and I lifted her up every single day. Losing Christian was not going to be part of my story, but I meet those who have faced tremendous loss everywhere I go. It's tempting to offer quick-and-easy verses to those who are in pain, but walking through the possibility of losing my son changed me. The tears I wept washed more than my face, they washed my soul.

I looked out of the plane window as we began our descent, hoping to catch my first glimpse of Winnipeg, Canada. According to the announcement from the pilot we were almost on the ground, which was hard to believe. All I could see was a thick layer of white clouds. As I stared more intently, however, I realized I wasn't looking at clouds; I was looking at snow. Everything was covered by a thick blanket of snow, as if Winnipeg had been tucked in for the night. I'd been invited to speak at a women's conference that weekend, and our host had advised me that it would be cold. As we stepped out of the plane and the first blast of frigid air hit my face, it became bitterly clear to me that the word *cold* is a relative term. There's "Would you like a cold beverage?" and then there is "Would you like your face to fall off in the next five minutes?"

I looked at the weather app on my phone and saw that it was 20 degrees below zero. Now that's cold. I made a comment about the temperature to the customs official as he looked at my passport (not a smart idea by the way), and he advised me, somewhat sternly, to be grateful, as it can get to forty below. I assured him that I was grateful—very, very grateful.

One of the members of the conference organizing committee picked Barry and me up and drove us to our hotel. I asked her if it was hard to drive in this weather as the roads were covered with a solid coat of ice. She assured me it wasn't as we skidded through a red light. She clearly lived with a glass-half-full mentality. I liked her immediately! We checked into our hotel and when I tried to open the drapes to see our view, the drapes were literally frozen to the window. I realize some of this might sound like an exaggeration; I promise you it's not. There's cold and then there's up-north-winter cold.

I got up at 6 AM the following morning to get ready. I plugged in my curling iron and attempted to curl my hair. I don't like it too curly, just a nice, soft, beachy wave, but it flatly refused to move. My hair had lost the will to live. I put on my leather pants and a long white silk shirt. The shirt immediately stuck to my skin as if it was having a panic attack. I took it off and, just out of curiosity, threw it at the wall. It stuck. I'd never encountered that degree of static electricity or bone-dry air before. Four hours north in a plane and I'd landed on another planet. I spritzed the shirt with water and put it back on. I piled on a jacket, then a coat, a scarf, and gloves and headed out into the bleak winter morning.

As we drove to the theater I looked over the day's schedule. It was jam-packed. They had apparently added a few extra things into the program. Women were driving from all over Canada, so they wanted to make it worth their while. I was now speaking four times, and then a question-and-answer session, an altar call, and finally leading the women in a communion service.

It was my first time in Winnipeg, but I hope it won't be my last. I fell in love with the women who came. They were warm (relatively speaking!) and eager to lean in and learn, with their Bibles, notebooks, and pens ready. The theater was packed to capacity, which seemed like the perfect way to hold in body heat—close fellowship of the survival kind. I spoke twice in the morning session, and then we broke for lunch. I'd never had a sandwich with frozen lettuce before (it gives the term *iceberg* a whole new meaning), so I decided to let it thaw out for a bit and meet some of the women one-on-one.

I'm always amazed at the strength of those who are walking through devastating times but still trusting God, even when their life makes no sense. A woman pulled out her cell phone to show me a picture of her son. I'll protect a few of the details to honor her privacy, but even as I looked into her eyes to comment on how handsome he was, I saw an ocean of sorrow. She had faced the unthinkable in any mother's life: having to bury her son.

The thought of that took my breath away. I had no words. All I could do was hold her and weep with her. She had come alone to the conference, which was titled "In the Middle of the Mess, Finding Strength for This Beautiful, Broken Life." I imagine that the only word that made sense to her was *broken*. Life was not beautiful. She didn't even want strength. She was broken. This was never the life she imagined. I was afraid to speak a word to her. What could I possibly say that would touch the depth of her pain? In what felt like a holy moment, she hugged me and through bitter tears said, "Thank you." I have no idea what God gave her that day. I had read this passage from Hebrews: "Therefore, since we are surrounded by so great a cloud of witnesses, let us also lay aside every weight, and sin which clings so closely, and let us run with endurance the race that is set before us, looking to Jesus, the founder and perfecter of our faith, who for the joy that was set before him endured the cross, despising the shame, and is seated at the right hand of the throne of God" (12:1–2 ESV).

In my humanity I wondered how any of these words could find her through the maze of her pain. I was reminded again that God's Word is a living love letter, not simply words on a page: it's alive. The Holy Spirit had taken truth and poured salve onto a broken heart. It's a mystery to me.

Every time before I speak, I get down on my knees and ask God to do what only He can do. When I first look out at a room of smiling faces I've no idea what's going on deep inside, but He does, and by the power of the Holy Spirit miracles happen. In those profound moments I'm always reminded of the story where Christ fed five thousand people on a hillside. The account is in all four Gospels, but Mark gives a detail that the others miss. Understanding that one simple detail, the question Christ asks His friends has shifted my entire perspective on ministry.

> Jesus saw the huge crowd as he stepped from the boat, and he had compassion on them because they were like sheep without a shepherd. So he began teaching them many things.
>
> Late in the afternoon his disciples came to him and said, "This is a remote place, and it's already getting late. Send the crowds away so they can go to the nearby farms and villages and buy something to eat."
>
> But Jesus said, "You feed them."
>
> "With what?" they asked. "We'd have to work for months to earn enough money to buy food for all these people!"
>
> "How much bread do you have?" he asked. "Go and find out."
>
> They came back and reported, "We have five loaves of bread and two fish." (Mark 6:34–38)

In biblical times, only the men were counted in a crowd, so if you had five thousand men there must have been at least nine or ten thousand people, adding in women and children. That's an arena-size crowd. Do you think in a crowd of that size the only food available was the little boy's lunch? I don't think so. If there were women on the hillside that day, there were snacks. Women are always prepared with something in case their children get hungry and start making a fuss. I imagine that no one else offered up their food, either because they didn't think it would be enough or they didn't want to share. The only one to give what he had was the little boy with five small barley loaves and two little fish. He gave what was clearly not enough and then Jesus did what only He can do.

Jesus took the five loaves and two fish, looked up toward heaven, and blessed them. Then, breaking the loaves into pieces, he kept giving the bread to the disciples so they could distribute it to the people. He also divided the fish for everyone to share. They all ate as much as they wanted, and afterward, the disciples picked up twelve baskets of leftover bread and fish. A total of 5,000 men and their families were fed. (vv. 41–44)

It was a miracle on the hillside that day, but the principle applies to us as well. We'll never have enough to fulfill all the demands made on us, but that's okay. We're not supposed to have enough. We're supposed to bring what we have, our clearly *not enough,* to Jesus and ask Him to meet us where we are.

When we give Jesus our *not enough* He blesses it and breaks it and He feeds His people. Understanding that principle has shifted something deep inside me. I will never have enough to touch the needs of everyone in a crowd, whether it's a crowd of fifty or a crowd of ten thousand. But I'm not asked to. Jesus simply asks me, "What do you have?" It was clear to me that afternoon in Winnipeg, Canada, that once more I was like that little boy on the hillside who got to watch a miracle. This wasn't the kind of miracle that would make a good movie or the kind we often wish for. In those stories, everyone gets fed, everyone gets healed, and all marriages are restored. What I saw that day was the presence of Christ showing up in the middle of devastating disappointment and holding someone who could barely stand. Just as I brought the little I had to the table, so did that brave mom. She got up that morning, washed her face, got dressed, and made it by herself to join a crowd of sisters, trusting that Christ would meet her with the little she was able to bring—and He did. Her simple act of getting up and putting one foot in front of the other was an act of worship.

I love this detail that John includes as he tells the same story:

Then Jesus took the loaves, gave thanks to God, and distributed them to the people. (John 6:11)

Jesus thanked His Father for the *not enough* given up by one little boy. The spiritual principle of bringing the little we have and trusting Christ to meet us there applies across all areas of life, not just in what we perceive as ministry situations. I look at all of life as ministry, twenty-four hours a day, seven days a week. It's become a daily habit of mine to acknowledge every morning that I don't have enough for the challenges that day will hold, and I ask Christ to meet me there. When you and I do that, Christ gives thanks. In our humanity we are bowing the knee to our Lord and Savior and acknowledging that He is God and we are not. To offer up the little we have in faith is a gift to Jesus. I find it significant that once the crowd had eaten as much as they wanted, there were twelve baskets left over, one for each disciple. These were not the delicate little baskets that we put dinner rolls in. These were the large baskets that Roman soldiers kept their swords in. It's as if Jesus is saying to His closest friends, "Do you get it now? Do you understand? You'll never have enough, but that's not the point. In Me there is more than enough."

There are so many places where we need the grace of an everyday miracle. Are you struggling as a mom? Perhaps you have three kids all needing to be at different places at the same time and it's overwhelming. Many days you feel frustrated. Some days you feel like a failure.

Do you struggle in your job? Your boss has unreasonably high expectations that you can't live up to, so you constantly feel stressed and anxious. That kind of pressure is paralyzing. Rather than encouraging the best that is in you, the message is that no matter what you do, it won't be enough. It's hard to rise above that.

Are you struggling with your health? You think back to days when life was different, and you could do so much more. Now you feel as if you have little to offer.

Whatever it is that you're facing right now, Christ invites you to bring who you are and what you have or don't have to Him in honesty and humility and wait with Him there.

We're not supposed

to have *enough.*

We're supposed to bring

what we have,

our clearly not enough,

to Jesus and ask Him

to *meet us* where we are.

Lord, I don't have enough energy, I don't have enough time, I don't have enough money. I don't have enough patience, I'm not enough.

As we wait before Him, the invitation comes:

Come to me, all of you who are weary and carry heavy burdens, and I will give you rest. Take my yoke upon you. Let me teach you, because I am humble and gentle at heart, and you will find rest for your souls. For my yoke is easy to bear, and the burden I give you is light. (Matt. 11:28–30)

A yoke is something that is laid over the shoulders of two oxen. They bear the weight together. Christ's invitation to us is greater. He will walk beside us and carry the weight.

I used to question God when I met someone who was in as much pain as the mom who had recently buried her son. How could God allow these things to happen? I struggled because I used my human understanding to try to understand the divine plans and ways of God. I'll never know enough about Him this side of eternity to make everything crystal clear. So I don't question anymore. Instead, I pray for them, often with tears running down my face, and I worship God in that sacred space of not understanding. That may seem like a strange response. It could come across like a cultlike obedience that's out of touch with reality. Far from it. For me, there is no greater reality than the love and faithfulness of God. I don't always see God's hand in a heartbreaking situation but as the great preacher Charles Spurgeon wrote, "And when we cannot trace His hand, we must trust His heart."[1]

Think about it this way: I'm not living by faith if I have an answer to everything. If I understand everything God does or doesn't do, then all I need to love Him with is my mind. We're called to love Him with more. When an expert in religious law asked Christ what he had to do to inherit eternal life, Christ asked him what his understanding was from the laws given to Moses. His response was,

"You must love the LORD your God with all your heart, all your soul, all your strength, and all your mind." And, "Love your neighbor as yourself." (Luke 10:27)

Christ told him he'd answered correctly. Heart, soul, strength, and mind. What does that look like for you and me right now? We love with our heart, even when it's broken. We love with our soul, even when our humanity wrestles against our situation. We love with our strength, even when it's almost gone. We love with our mind, even when we don't understand.

If you know anything of my story, you know I don't say these things flippantly. I say them with faith, believing 100 percent as deep as the marrow in my bones that God is good and we can trust Him even when we don't understand where we are in life. As Paul wrote to the church in Corinth, "Now we see things imperfectly, like puzzling reflections in a mirror, but then we will see everything with perfect clarity" (1 Cor. 13:12).

At most of my conferences we have time for a question-and-answer session. I get the usual one or two cute ones:

Where did you meet your husband?
Where did you get your boots?

Others are harder to read:

I'm facing cancer for the second time. Why would God allow this?
I was sexually abused as a child, twice by different members of my family. I don't know what to do with the shame.

There is always a common thread to the questions I get: *Life is disappointing. This is not the life I imagined.* I think most of us could say that. Think back to when you were a teenager. What did you imagine your life would look like? I thought I was going to be a nurse until I discovered that it meant being around blood. Perhaps you thought you'd get married and have lots of children or you saw yourself as a career woman running your own business one day. When I was in seminary, one of the girls who became my friend told me that in her application form, when asked where she believed God was calling her, she had written, "Pastor's wife. Pastor not found yet."

Some unexpected changes in life are welcome, but no one imagines the hard things that wait just around the corner. How do we live, then, when we find ourselves in a place that's far from the life we imagined? When I consider a woman from Scripture who could state unequivocally that the life she was living was not the one she dreamed of, I think of Abigail. We find her story in 1 Samuel 25, weaved into the time when David was running for his life from King Saul. I love the lessons of her life. We get to see someone living in a difficult situation yet whose wisdom and faithfulness to God guided her in the midst of her disappointment and eventually brought her into a whole new space of grace. Her name means "My Father Is Joy." I believe that's where she found her strength, because her husband, Nabal, brought no joy to Abigail's life. His name meant "fool," and he lived up to it.

Standing Strong When Dreams Are Deferred

> Then David moved down to the wilderness of Maon. There was a wealthy man from Maon who owned property near the town of Carmel. He had 3,000 sheep and 1,000 goats, and it was sheep-shearing time. This man's name was Nabal, and his wife, Abigail, was a sensible and beautiful woman. But Nabal, a descendant of Caleb, was crude and mean in all his dealings. (1 Sam. 25:1–3)

In those days women had little say in whom they married. Nabal, a wealthy man, must have seemed like a good catch to Abigail's father, but money is never enough to guarantee a peaceful life. I wonder how many days it took before she realized what kind of man she was married to? I imagine not too many. He is described as "crude and mean in all his dealings." I'm sure he treated her that way. Not only that, Abigail had to watch him treat everyone who worked for him that way as well. He was a cruel man. It's hard to see the ugly underbelly of someone you believe you once loved. Nabal drank a lot, often got drunk, and, in that state, became even more disgusting.

Even in our day where we get to choose who we'll hopefully spend the rest of our lives with, our true selves often don't emerge until that band of gold is on our finger. We can hide our brokenness when we're dating, but when the dailiness of life kicks in, it can rear its ugly head. I don't think Barry understood what it meant to live with someone who has a diagnosis of clinical depression when we first married. Not only that, I didn't know how to let someone into that place I had guarded so carefully. Barry had his issues too, and it took us years of learning to trust each other and to trust God in each other. At times we sought the advice of a good counselor and found a path to be able to know and love each other well.

No marriage is easy. All take hard work. But when only one party sees a problem or is willing to work on it, it's hard to move forward. I'm thinking of those of you who are in a difficult marriage right now. My heart aches for you. When you stand at the altar, or in front of a judge, the road ahead looks sunny and clear. When storm clouds begin to gather and the sky becomes as dark as night, it's hard to remember that happy couple who made their vows in front of God and family. Most times, the storm will pass. If you both learn from it, you're more prepared to weather the next one. But sometimes the storm is more like a tornado—wrecking everything in its path, changing the landscape of your life—and your marriage comes to an end. If that's your story, I'm so sorry. Whether you were the one who wanted the divorce or not, it's painful to rip two lives apart. In those times we need to hold on to the truth that when hearts are broken, He is close. When we are crushed, Christ is near. You are not alone.

When you give up on yourself, God does not. What I want us to see in Abigail's story, however, applies to all of us—married, single, or divorced. She was a woman living in a desperately disappointing situation, but clearly, she didn't allow it to change who she was. Somehow Abigail was able to be okay in a situation that was not okay. But there was one life-altering day when everything came to a head, and she was the only hope between two men. One was a foolish, arrogant man and one was a powerful, angry man.

David was on the run from King Saul. Saul had lost the ability to hear the voice of God, and his jealousy over David's popularity had pushed him to the edge of sanity. (Read more of the story in 1 Sam. 15–19.) The only thing on the mind of the king was killing David, not serving the people. So David ran from the palace, and he and six hundred men took refuge in the desert of Maon, close to where Abigail and Nabal lived. Since they had settled there, all of Nabal's flocks had been kept safe from the thieves who had been stealing from him. His flocks were now thriving and his wealth increasing. So David sent a message to Nabal.

> When David heard that Nabal was shearing his sheep, he sent ten of his young men to Carmel with this message for Nabal: "Peace and prosperity to you, your family, and everything you own! I am told that it is sheep-shearing time. While your shepherds stayed among us near Carmel, we never harmed them, and nothing was ever stolen from them. Ask your own men, and they will tell you this is true. So would you be kind to us, since we have come at a time of celebration? Please share any provisions you might have on hand with us and with your friend David." (1 Sam. 25:4–8)

Nice note. Respectful, yet pointing out that as it's now sheep-shearing time, Nabal might notice that he has more sheep to shear this year than last. David wasn't asking for a lot, just to share whatever food and other provisions Nabal might have on hand. A reasonable man would have been grateful to David and his men, but Nabal was not.

> "Who is this fellow David?" Nabal sneered to the young men. "Who does this son of Jesse think he is? There are lots of servants these days who run away from their masters. Should I take my bread and my water and my meat that I've slaughtered for my shearers and give it to a band of outlaws who come from who knows where?" (1 Sam. 25:10–11)

When the men returned to David and told him about Nabal's response, he was furious. He told four hundred of his men to get their swords ready and left the remaining two hundred behind to guard their equipment. His intention was to make sure that not one man in Nabal's household would be alive in the morning.

The next part of the story is fascinating and tells us a lot about Abigail. One of the servants who heard Nabal scream insults at David's men knew he had to do something, but he didn't talk to Nabal, he went to Abigail. That speaks volumes to me. Clearly those around her had been watching Abigail. You wouldn't have to be a rocket scientist to know that her life was difficult. The servants must have heard how Nabal talked to her, saw how he treated her. More significant than that, they saw who she was despite the way she was treated. Even though she was living a life that was clearly not the life any woman would have chosen, she was kind and strong. His cruelty had not changed her character.

I've had to sit with that for a while and ask myself, *How would I have been in those circumstances?* I'm not sure I would have had her grace. It would be hard not to become disillusioned or bitter living with someone who was mean and foolish day after day. She clearly was not. What she does next shows us the kind of woman she was. Abigail packed as much food and wine as she could and set out to meet David. I've tried to put myself in her shoes and imagine what I would have said. I think it would have gone a little like this: *I am so, so sorry. Please forgive us. My husband is a moron.*

That was not how Abigail began. Her carefully worded speech is one of the longest recorded from any woman in Scripture, and it is masterful. She begins this way: "I accept all blame in this matter, my lord" (1 Sam. 25:24).

What? What a way to begin. None of what happened was Abigail's fault, but she is a wise woman. She knows that her humility and respect might begin to lower the level of rage in David. But before you start to think that she's a weak, codependent wife defending a useless husband who has clearly endangered the lives of all around him, she continues:

> Please listen to what I have to say. I know Nabal is a wicked and ill-tempered man; please don't pay any attention to him. He is a fool, just as his name suggests. But I never even saw the young men you sent.
>
> Now, my lord, as surely as the LORD lives and you yourself live, since the LORD has kept you from murdering and taking vengeance into your own hands, let all your enemies and those who try to harm you be as cursed as Nabal is. And here is a present that I, your servant, have brought to you and your young men. Please forgive me if I have offended you in any way. The LORD will surely reward you with a lasting dynasty, for you are fighting the LORD's battles. And you have not done wrong throughout your entire life.
>
> Even when you are chased by those who seek to kill you, your life is safe in the care of the LORD your God, secure in his treasure pouch! But the lives of your enemies will disappear like stones shot from a sling! When the LORD has done all he promised and has made you leader of Israel, don't let this be a blemish on your record. Then your conscience won't have to bear the staggering burden of needless bloodshed and vengeance. And when the LORD has done these great things for you, please remember me, your servant! (vv. 24–31)

Not only did Abigail make it clear that she knew who her husband was, more importantly, she told David that she knew who he was. She reminded him that he was called to fight the Lord's battles, not those stirred up by a foolish man. A fool can bring out the worst in us and make us forget who we are. When we react impulsively we often regret it. Abigail redirected David's eyes to God, and he blessed her for that.

Thank God for your good sense! Bless you for keeping me from murder and from carrying out vengeance with my own hands. (v. 33)

I want to be a woman like that. One who doesn't react but is able to respond. One who reminds those around me of who and whose we are. It's so easy to be pulled down by the out-of-control behavior of others. We can apply this lesson in so many situations. Do you work with someone who makes you roll your eyes and pray that God will move them on? If you do, will you choose to stay above the foolishness? Others are watching you, taking a lead from you. Perhaps there's someone in your church or Bible study who is mean and unkind to everyone. The temptation is to react, to form our own little group and hit back. Abigail challenges us to acknowledge what's true, to confront with truth when that's called for, but also to remain who we are in Christ and call those around us to do the same.

When Abigail got home that night, Nabal was drunk. Rather than try to reason with a drunken fool, she waited until the next morning. When she told Nabal what she had done, his heart failed him. He either had a heart attack or a stroke, and ten days later, he died.

When David heard that Nabal had died, he asked Abigail to marry him. Quite a dramatic story. She had endured a lot. You may not be married to a Nabal or waiting for a David, but I know that there are disappointments in life, dreams that fall by the wayside, but as the Scripture at the beginning of this chapter reminds us, when we choose by faith to press on, to endure in Christ then endurance produces strength of character, and character produces a confident hope of salvation. And that hope, that assurance that whether some dreams may have to fall by the wayside on this earth, our true hope in Christ will not disappoint.

Not all disappointments are born out of tragedy, of course. Many are simply dreams deferred or finding ourselves in a new season of life.

New Seasons, New Dreams, New Possibilities

A long time ago I attended a church where the pastor's wife and I became friends. I think she saw me as a bit of an odd duck and decided to waddle beside me. As we became closer, she told me that she loved her husband but was miserable in her current situation. The other women expected her to be what the last pastor's wife had been. She had been a confident speaker and leader who loved to host women's events. These were not the same gifts as my friend possessed. She was quiet but had a deeply compassionate heart. I could see that she was being suffocated by the mold she was expected to fill. One day I asked her if she could design the life she imagined, what would that look like? She said that she'd love to reach women who would never come to church, those who felt they would not be welcome.

"Sounds good!" I said. "Let's pray together to see that dream find wings."

A few years later her husband was called to pastor an inner-city church, and finally my friend found the place where her passion intersected with a profound need. Every Friday and Saturday night, she and a group of like-minded women from her new church prepared sandwiches and hot coffee and took it to an area in downtown known for prostitution. I bumped into her one day, several months after their move, and I couldn't believe the physical difference in her. It was as if the weight of the world had been rolled off her back. Her eyes lit up as she told me what it was like to be able to look into the eyes of a woman who felt little self-worth and tell her she was loved by God. I asked her if she was ever afraid to walk those streets at night. She said she wasn't, because she knew she was where God had designed her to be. It took a lot of time for my friend to be able to finally use the gifts that God had placed in her. When that dream was finally realized it was all the sweeter.

We've looked at a mom who experienced tragedy, a woman married to a fool, and one feeling forced into a role that didn't fit. The question is, How does this relate to your life right now? You may never face any of those specific situations, but what can we take from each one of them to strengthen us, to help us move forward?

The common denominator woven through each story is struggle and disappointment. We've watered down the word *disappointment* in our culture. Now we're disappointed if they discontinue our favorite shade of lipstick or if a movie didn't live up to the advertising hype. The word has greater weight. The synonyms for disappointment are *sadness*, *regret*, *sorrow*, or *loss*. We all face those at different times in our lives. Not all losses are huge. Some we even saw coming—but it didn't make them any easier.

In 2015 our only son went off to college. Barry and I drove with him to College Station, Texas, to get him settled into the new apartment he was sharing with one of his best friends. We were so happy for him. He'd been accepted into his first choice of school, Texas A&M, and he was ready to begin this new chapter in his life. We stayed for a couple of days and then headed home. About ten minutes into the trip I started to cry. I cried the whole three hours home. I kept apologizing to Barry, saying that I was fine. I just couldn't stop crying. "I'm happy for him, honestly!" I said, choking back the sobs. We finally made it home without drowning. I went into the kitchen to get dinner ready, and Barry said he'd take a shower. When our meal was ready, I went to look for him. He wasn't in the shower or in our room. I found him in Christian's room, lying on his bed, sobbing. When he saw me he said, "I'm happy for him, I really am!"

We all face change. Some of it we welcome, and some we don't look forward to. The thing that will keep us strong and help us move forward is knowing that Christ is with us and for us, and the hope we have in Him ultimately will not disappoint. Perhaps you can take a few moments today and ask the Holy Spirit to show you places of disappointment in your life. Some of them might even be from your childhood but are still casting a shadow today. Write them down, and then let your Father know that these hurt. He already knows, but sometimes we need to be reminded that He knows. Like that little boy on the hillside, offer what you have up to Jesus. This is an act of worship that He will receive.

The thing that
will keep us *strong*
and help us move forward

is knowing that Christ

is with us and for us,

and the *hope* we have

in Him ultimately

will not disappoint.

One Step at a Time

We're Not Enough, but Jesus Is

1. Be brutally honest. Be honest with yourself about the areas of your life that are disappointing. That can be hard to do, because some of them can't be changed and it may feel like acknowledging them will only make the burden harder to bear. That would be true if you had to bear it alone. Christ invites you to share it with Him. Write them down. Face them. Talk to God about them. Talk to God about the areas where you feel hopeless and disappointed. Ask Jesus to walk with you in the places that are hard.

2. Ask God to help you dream a new dream. Is there something you always wanted to do but it got pushed to the back burner because of everything else in life? Go to a local nursery and get a packet of seeds and a little pot. Look at the seeds when you get home. They don't look like much. Plant and water them and then watch for the first signs of life. What are the little seeds in your heart that, with care and watering in prayer, might give birth to something new?

3. Meditate on this verse:

   > Truly, truly, I say to you, unless a grain of wheat falls into the earth and dies, it remains alone; but if it dies, it bears much fruit. (John 12:24 ESV)

   Sometimes we have to let one dream die to welcome a new one.

seven

Celebrate Your Scars
as Tattoos of Triumph

That Sunday evening the disciples were meeting behind locked doors because they were afraid of the Jewish leaders. Suddenly, Jesus was standing there among them! "Peace be with you," he said. As he spoke, he showed them the wounds in his hands and his side. They were filled with joy when they saw the Lord!

—John 20:19–20

He will be known by the scars.

—Michael Card,
Known by the Scars (1983)

I read a comment someone left on my Facebook page one day and it made me smile. The person had written, "I pray that one day I can be the fearless godly woman you are."

I sent off a brief reply, aware that it didn't come close to telling the whole story of what a fear-filled child and young woman I had been and the long, hard walk to understand where true courage is found. Because I have a public ministry, people tend to see the battles I've won, but they don't always see the number of times I've had to run home and fall at the feet of Jesus, exhausted and empty. I love the promise of Psalm 91: "He will cover you with His wings. And under His wings you will be safe. He is faithful like a safe-covering and a strong wall" (v. 4).

I wished I could sit with this person and walk through the years of my life and the moments that had shaped me, but where would I even start? Do photos tell the story?

I treasure an old black-and-white photo taken in my parents' garden before my dad's death. My mum, shiny black hair falling in gentle curls onto her shoulders, sweet smile, holding my sister's hand. Me, sitting on a blanket on the grass, my handsome dad kneeling behind me as I lean on him for support. I must have been about two years old, and from the shape of my face I was clearly being well fed. (Little known fact: When I was born, I was ten pounds. That's a turkey!) It's a happy photo. We all look so happy.

Fast-forward four years. Something has changed in the photo of my six-year-old self. I'm standing in a blue dress with the summer sun kissing my face with freckles. I'm smiling but there's a guardedness in my smile. I see it in my shoulders too; no longer leaning into the photo, I'm pulling slightly back.

Then there are highlights from later in life. I have a photo with the Queen's daughter, Princess Anne. I was hosting a Royal Gala performance of various pop stars and actors in London's Royal Albert Hall for the princess's favorite charity, Save the Children. The photographer snapped it backstage just as I was curtsying, so I look like a garden gnome. As I look at it now though it's quite glamorous. A young British designer had outfitted me for the performance with a beautiful black sparkly jacket and pants. One of the makeup artists from the British Broadcasting Company, the BBC, had done my makeup, as the show was being televised. I'm sure if I showed my Facebook friend that photo she would think I'd overcome the pain of my childhood and now stood fearless on that stage. But I remember how I felt inside that night. I felt disconnected, alone, as if I watched life from the safety of a self-constructed glass cage.

What about the Polaroid taken the night I was admitted to the psychiatric hospital—pale, thin, eyes dim as if the lights had been turned off inside? Does that tell a more honest story? Or do our scars tell the story?

Should I start with the little indentation on my right knee? I fell off my bike when I was four and Mum had to dig the gravel out. I was so proud of that scar. I showed it to my dad as if I was presenting him with a medal I'd won in the war. My sister told me to stop picking at it as it would get bigger. I told her that was the whole point.

What about the scar on my upper left arm from the mandatory vaccinations every Scottish child was given in school? They called it the "bird's nest" because it was round and had five little needles, little birds that popped up and stabbed you. I remember lining up behind my classmates in the nurse's room. They were chatting and laughing, but I was terrified. By this point in my life, I associated any type of pain with overwhelming loss. I wanted no more scars.

None of these pictures or scars would tell the turning point in my story. No picture could capture that profound moment when, finally, the scars of Christ met the woundedness in me. For that, I would have to take her to the back row of a small church in Washington, DC, in 1992. I had been in the psychiatric hospital for three weeks, and my doctor wanted me to take a trip outside the hospital walls with one of the nurses. He suggested I might like to go to the mall or a movie. I said no; I wanted to go to a church. It didn't matter the denomination, just a Bible-believing church. I sat in the back row that Sunday morning, dead to the powerful words of the hymns, watching the sun streaming through the stained-glass windows, yet feeling cold inside.

The *scars* of Christ

met the

woundedness

in me.

Have you ever been in a place like that, a place where you felt so hopeless that no matter what anyone said, it didn't reach you? Have you ever looked at words that used to bring life and joy and hope when you opened the Word of God, and now they're just words on a page? Have you ever felt that even when you're surrounded by people, you are desperately alone?

That's where I was that September morning, alone and lost. I don't remember the message. I found it hard to concentrate. But as the pastor came to the end of his message he said something that caught my attention. He said that he knew some of us felt dead inside. I looked up. It was like he was talking to me. He said, no matter how deep the hole was, Jesus was here. He went on to say that we didn't have to get ourselves out of the hole, just call on His name and He would be the one to pull us free. In that moment, I felt as if I was the only one in the church; even the pastor was gone. The only one standing there, arms open wide, with nail-pierced hands, was Jesus. I don't even remember if the service was over as I ran to the front of the church and lay facedown before a simple wooden cross. The words of a hymn that my beloved nana used to sing to me when I was a child washed over me in healing waves:

> Rock of Ages, cleft for me,
> Let me hide myself in Thee;
> Let the water and the blood,
> From Thy wounded side which flowed,
> Be of sin the double cure,
> Save from wrath and make me pure.
>
> Not the labor of my hands
> Can fulfill Thy law's demands;
> Could my zeal no respite know,
> Could my tears forever flow,
> All for sin could not atone;
> Thou must save, and Thou alone.

Nothing in my hands I bring
Simply to thy cross I cling
Naked, come to Thee for dress;
Helpless, look to Thee for grace;
Foul, I to the fountain fly;
Wash me, Savior, or I die.[1]

Something deep began in my life that day. It was an understanding that God's love and acceptance of me had never been about me being good enough or pretty enough or strong enough. I saw that the One with scarred hands invited me to come out of that glass cage in all my brokenness and be seen. I realized that day how much of my life had been spent in hiding. The irony for me was that so much of my hiding took place in public. Although as an adult I knew that the anger my father took out on me before his suicide was because of his brain damage, the messages I internalized as a child had lived with me for years.

If your own dad could eventually hate you, anyone could.

Don't let anyone get too close or they might see what he saw.

Help other people so they see you have a purpose and won't reject you.

It's possible to do a lot of right things for the wrong reasons. As I left the church that morning I knew I wasn't fixed, but I was seen— seen in all my brokenness, and loved. If Christ had chosen to live eternally with His scars, why would I be ashamed to show mine?

I have a new scar that I treasure now. It resulted from two recent surgeries. The first is a horizontal scar on my belly where one of my ovaries was removed. The grapefruit-sized tumor was benign, but the surgery left quite a long horizontal scar. A couple years later I had that second surgery on my back. As I mentioned earlier, the surgeon apologized upfront for the shape his vertical incision

If Christ had chosen

to live eternally

with His *scars*,

why would I be ashamed

to *show mine?*

would leave. However, I didn't realize until it began to heal what image the second scar had created. As it was healing, I discovered that I am permanently marked by a cross. I love these scars. I love them because they are a physical reminder to me every day that Christ is permanently scarred for you and me. He didn't hide His scars and neither will I.

God Tells His Story in Scars

> Can a woman forget her nursing child,
> > that she should have no compassion on the son of her
> > womb?
> Even these may forget,
> > yet I will not forget you.
> Behold, I have engraved you on the palms of my hands;
> > your walls are continually before me. (Isa. 49:15–16 ESV)

The Hebrew word for "engraved" is *chaqaq*. It means "to be cut into or cut open." The practice of having an image on the palms of your hands was a familiar one to Jews. The practice was called "ensigns of Jerusalem." Jewish men would engrave pictures of the temple or of Jerusalem on the palms of their hands. It meant for the devout Jew that these images would be always before them. This is what they did. They would choose an image and then have it cut into a block of wood. Then they'd dip the image into powder or charcoal and apply it to the palms of their hands. Next, they would tie two needles tightly together and dip them into ink, then gently pierce along the image, careful not to draw blood. When the image was complete it would be washed in wine. It reminded them of the temple, but not of the Lamb of God who takes away the sin of the world. They still had to follow the laws given to Moses. They still had to have an animal sacrificed, symbolically taking their sins away. They had to do this over and over. But the prophet Isaiah spoke of the One to come who would step into our place and once for all take our punishment on Himself:

> Surely he has borne our griefs
> and carried our sorrows;
> yet we esteemed him stricken,
> smitten by God, and afflicted.
> But he was pierced for our transgressions;
> he was crushed for our iniquities;
> upon him was the chastisement that brought us peace,
> and with his wounds we are healed. (Isa. 53:4–5 ESV)

I remember as a child being told in Sunday school that God had our names inscribed into the palms of His hands and wondering how big His hands would have to be to fit us all in. Now I think that every time God the Father sees the pierced hands of Christ, He sees you and me. There is no image that displays the love of God more perfectly than the scars of Jesus. The scars tell God's story.

> That Sunday evening the disciples were meeting behind locked doors because they were afraid of the Jewish leaders. Suddenly, Jesus was standing there among them! "Peace be with you," he said. As he spoke, he showed them the wounds in his hands and his side. They were filled with joy when they saw the Lord! (John 20:19–20)

I can only imagine what that day must have been like. For three years, these men had followed Jesus from town to town. They watched the crowds grow, saw miracles happen before their eyes. They had seen Jesus turn a storm into a sea of glass with a single word. They knew that any moment now Jesus would take His place in Jerusalem and overthrow the Roman government. It's important to remember what they knew of Scripture at that point. They didn't have what we have. All they had were the Old Testament scrolls. These had been read to them in the temple since they were children.

There is no image

that displays

the *love of God*

more perfectly than

the scars of *Jesus*.

Every Jew held on particularly to the promise of these words from the prophet Isaiah about the coming Messiah:

> For a child is born to us,
>   a son is given to us.
> The government will rest on his shoulders.
>   And he will be called:
> Wonderful Counselor, Mighty God,
>   Everlasting Father, Prince of Peace.
> His government and its peace
>   will never end.
> He will rule with fairness and justice from the throne of his
>   ancestor David
>   for all eternity.
> The passionate commitment of the LORD of Heaven's
>   Armies
>   will make this happen! (Isa. 9:6–7)

Think about it. If that's all you've heard since you were a child, then you would expect that if Jesus was indeed the Messiah, all those things were about to happen now. They had followed Jesus, watched Him do the things prophesied that Messiah would do, and now they were waiting for Christ to take over. When Jesus entered Jerusalem on a donkey and the crowds went wild throwing palm branches at His feet, they must have believed that the reign of Messiah was beginning. The story was beginning to unfold, but not the way they thought it would. John records much of that final conversation Jesus had with His disciples on the night He was betrayed. He tried to prepare them for what was about to happen, but they didn't understand.

> What does he mean when he says, "In a little while you won't see me, but then you will see me," and "I am going to the Father"? And what does he mean by "a little while"? We don't understand. (John 16:17–18)

Yet they were singing hymns that night as they left the upper room and headed across the Kidron Valley. Then it all started to go wrong. Haven't you been there? I know I have. You're in a great place, loving God, family intact, when suddenly something you didn't see coming happens, and you wonder where God is, and does He see what's going on? I'm thinking of the thousands of messages I've received over the years asking that question, "What went wrong?"

I could relay so many of the different situations to you, but the one that hits you hardest is yours. No matter what it was, you simply didn't see it coming. It might be relational or health, finances or future plans, but whatever it is, when it hits, and it feels wrong, it's hard not to panic. We all know we'll face challenges in life, but sometimes we're hit by something that feels as if the enemy has won. That's a frightening place to be. That must have been how the disciples felt that night.

The first thing they saw were flaming torches approaching them, the sound of boots on the ground, and then, Judas stepped out of the shadows and kissed Jesus on the cheek. I'm sure they never quite trusted him. Money always seemed to be disappearing, but no one expected this. Somehow that kiss on the cheek seemed to unlock the powers of hell and the soldiers and temple guards moved in to arrest Christ. I know that later that night Peter would deny he knew Jesus, but I think we sometimes forget what he did in the garden. When Peter saw what was happening he drew out his sword and sliced off the ear of the high priest's slave. Peter was ready to fight. They were vastly outnumbered by the soldiers, and Christ's friends were not warriors, they were fishermen. I think Peter was ready to die in the garden that night. So when Jesus told him to put his sword away, and He healed the slave, it made no sense. It must have felt like a slap in the face to a proud man like Peter. From that moment on, everything seemed out of control. Finally, after a mockery of a trial and a Roman flogging, all their dreams were nailed to a cross.

As Christ died, the very earth literally shook underneath their feet and night fell hard.

Mark tells us that when some of the women went to the tomb on that resurrection morning an angel told them that Jesus wasn't there, that He had risen from the dead. The angel instructed Mary to tell the disciples and Peter (how kind to let him know that despite his denying he knew Jesus, he was included) that Jesus had gone ahead of them to Galilee. It must have sounded too good to be true. Nothing made sense anymore. That evening they gathered together behind locked doors. Life wasn't safe or predictable now. If the Jewish leaders could take an innocent man and have Him crucified, were they next?

Suddenly, they all stopped talking.

> That Sunday evening the disciples were meeting behind locked doors because they were afraid of the Jewish leaders. Suddenly, Jesus was standing there among them! "Peace be with you," he said. As he spoke, he showed them the wounds in his hands and his side. They were filled with joy when they saw the Lord! (John 20:19–20)

Peace to you. Can you even begin to imagine the pure, unadulterated joy of that moment? They'd seen the bruised and battered body taken down from the cross and wrapped in linen that became as red as crimson. Now here He was, alive again. Have you ever wondered why Christ kept the scars after His resurrection? He could have chosen to rise without those signs of the brutal execution He had experienced. Perhaps one of the reasons was for his closest friends. They would have no doubt that this was Jesus, the Christ who had been crucified. The great preacher Charles Spurgeon put it this way:

> He said, "Behold my hands and feet, that it is, I, myself." It was to establish his identity, that he was the very same Jesus whom they had followed, whom at last they had deserted, whom they had beheld afar off crucified and slain, and whom they had carried to the tomb in the gloom of the evening; it was the very same Christ who was

now before them, and they might know it, for there was the seal of his sufferings upon him.[2]

As Christ held out His nail-pierced hands and wounded side, they were no longer marks of death, they were signs of the ultimate victory: declaring that death was overcome by the blood of the Lamb. Christ wears those scars in heaven as glorious trophies of the battle He has won. The only wound from this earth in eternity will be the scars of Christ.

I wonder what the angels thought when they saw the Holy One return, marked like this? I think it would only make the worship more intense, the praise even more glorious. The wonder of what God in Christ had been willing to do for those He loves.

These scars are trophies of grace. If you are ever tempted for a moment to doubt your worth, remember this: The only innocent one who ever lived is marked forever because He thought you were worth it. The same man who wrote the beautiful hymn "Rock of Ages" in the eighteenth century wrote this:

> My name from the palms of His hands
> Eternity will not erase;
> Imprest on His heart it remains
> In marks of indelible grace.
>
> —Augustus Toplady

Do You Want to Get Well?

As the incisions from any surgery heal, it becomes clear that you no longer have wounds, you have scars. Scars tell us that we are healed, but sometimes, just as I did when I was four, we keep picking at them and they become open wounds again. My husband Barry has a little scar on the side of his cheek that he's been picking at for the last year. It drives me bonkers. Initially, he said that it was an ingrown hair, so he needed to pick at it to free the hair. That was months ago! Now I see him looking at it in the magnifying mirror in our bathroom every night. It has almost healed so many times, but then he'll pick at it again. When I ask him why he won't leave his poor, lovely face alone he'll say that he's sure that there's something still in there. My thought is, if there is something still in there, it's got to be dead by now!

Not long ago we were in Myrtle Beach, South Carolina, for a conference. We ended up with a free afternoon and headed to the beach. I love being by the water. It's my happy place. I find it so peaceful. Barry loves it too because he has a theory. He believes that salt water can heal anything. It's his version of Windex (*My Big Fat Greek Wedding* reference). We parked our rental car and walked down onto the sand. I stood for a few minutes with my eyes closed, listening to the sound of the waves and thanking God for the gift of a few hours by the ocean. When I opened my eyes, there he was, knee deep in the water, scooping it up in his hands and putting it on the side of his face. I assumed now that he was "healed" he'd leave it alone, but no. Every night, there he is pick, pick, picking.

Christian and I love to tease him about this, but there are far more serious situations when we don't want our wounds to heal. We don't want to lose them because they have become our identity. Jesus stands with open, nail-scarred hands reaching toward each one of us, but He won't force healing on us. We get to choose.

Inside the city, near the Sheep Gate, was the pool of Bethesda, with five covered porches. Crowds of sick people—blind, lame, or paralyzed—lay on the porches. One of the men lying there had been sick for thirty-eight years. When Jesus saw him and knew he had been ill for a long time, he asked him, "Would you like to get well?"

"I can't, sir," the sick man said, "for I have no one to put me into the pool when the water bubbles up. Someone else always gets there ahead of me."

Jesus told him, "Stand up, pick up your mat, and walk!" (John 5:2–8)

You can still see the pool of Bethesda today if you visit Israel. It's near the Church of St. Anne, in the northeast quarter of the old city. *Bethesda* means "house of mercy," or "house of outpouring." That's what those who gathered inside the five large covered porches longed for. They believed miracles happened there. When an angel stirred the waters, the first one into the pool would be healed.

I can't imagine how heartbreaking it would be to be an observer in that place when the waters stirred. Those who were waiting were blind, crippled, and desperately sick. If one person made a move toward the waters others must have done everything in their power to drag their poor, broken bodies to the edge of the pool, but only one would be healed. I imagine that this was a place most people avoided. It was a place of misery and disease, and Jewish people had such strict laws concerning who was clean and who was unclean. I love that Jesus chose to go there. He never stayed in the nicest places in town and seldom hung out with the most respectable crowd. He went to the poor and the broken, those whom society had given up on.

Some of those waiting for a miracle had friends to help them into the water, but the man Jesus talked to had no one. Perhaps he still came because he felt more at home among those who were as broken as he was. Jesus asked him what seems to be a strange question: "Would you like to get well?" Why would the man be there if he didn't want to get well? I've wondered, though, what this man's picture of God was like. He had been coming there for thirty-eight years, and it must have seemed that the grace of God was on a first-come, first-served basis. Perhaps Jesus chose him because he'd been there longer than anyone else. He had watched as time after time someone else got the miracle they wanted, and he didn't even get close. By this point in his life he'd pretty much given up hope. When Jesus asked him if he wanted to get well, his answer was that he couldn't.

Someone else always gets there before me.

He'd given up hope and accepted who he was—the one who never gets a miracle. The wound was always open.

I've wondered sometimes if there are situations where we find our identity in being wounded instead of scarred? That may sound harsh, but I've seen it many times. Unless we have a deep sense of the identity we are offered in our scar-marked Savior, we find our identity in our wounds.

You and I know that terrible things happen in this world. Children are sexually abused, wives are beaten, men lose their wives to breast cancer or find themselves out of a job at an age when it will be hard to find another. The list is long and hard. When we come to faith in Christ, we are offered healing and hope. This is never a quick fix. It can take years to begin to walk away from the things that wounded us so deeply, but as we continue to walk with Christ, His presence becomes greater than the wound and a scar forms. Our scars are proof that God heals. For some, however, the wound has given them identity, a story, one they're not willing to give up. The wound becomes the thing that is most true about them.

Christ wants more for us. He wants us to be whole. His words to the man by the pool that day were strong. The ESV translates chapter 5, verses 8–9, this way:

"Get up, take up your bed, and walk." And at once the man was healed, and he took up his bed and walked.

The original Greek is this:

Egeire! [Get up!]

This wasn't a suggestion. It was a command. It was with power and a foreshadowing of the days to come:

Truly, truly, I say to you, an hour is coming, and is now here, when the dead will hear the voice of the Son of God, and those who hear will live. (John 5:25 ESV)

The man stood up, and he was healed. He's an interesting character, though. He doesn't seem particularly grateful to be healed. When the Jewish religious leaders asked him why he was carrying his mat on the Sabbath, he pointed off in the distance and said, "That man told me to!" They asked him what man he was referring to, but he didn't know. He hadn't even bothered to ask Jesus what His name was. Later, Jesus confronted him in the temple. He'd known how long this man had been sick and He also knew what was in his heart, so He told him to stop sinning. Instead of falling on his knees in worship, he found the religious leaders and told them the man's name was Jesus. This man got up and walked, but he didn't follow Jesus. Miracles will never change us; obedience to Christ does that.

Invisible Scars

Not all scars are visible. Sometimes the scars we bear are from the choices we've made. Those are easier to hide, but they leave a mark inside. I think those scars are potentially the deadliest because they can't be seen, but the ongoing impact on our lives is profound.

King David knew what unconfessed sin does to the soul and the spirit. His hidden scars haunted him, day and night. You can read the specifics of that part of his story in 2 Samuel 11–12. The bottom line is that he slept with another man's wife. When she became pregnant, he sent her husband into the front line of a battle where David knew he would be killed. Adultery and murder. God had given David everything. The kingdom of Israel had never been larger. They were now living in the fullness of all the land that had been promised to Moses and their wealth was unprecedented. Having it all doesn't protect us from sin. David looked out one day and saw Bathsheba bathing. He wanted her, so he took her. God sent the prophet Nathan to confront him with his sin, and David finally broke down. He wrote Psalm 51 about the impact his sin had on his life.

Miracles

will never change us;

obedience to Christ

does that.

Purify me from my sins, and I will be clean;
    wash me, and I will be whiter than snow.
Oh, give me back my joy again;
    you have broken me—
    now let me rejoice.
Don't keep looking at my sins.
    Remove the stain of my guilt.
Create in me a clean heart, O God.
    Renew a loyal spirit within me.
Do not banish me from your presence,
    and don't take your Holy Spirit from me.

Restore to me the joy of your salvation,
    and make me willing to obey you. (vv. 7–12)

David was haunted by the secret scars inside. There was no joy, no rest, no hope. He knew what it looked like when the Holy Spirit leaves a person. He had seen that in King Saul. David recognized that although he had sinned against Bathsheba and Uriah, her husband, the real person he had sinned against was God. He gives us a template for when we've made the biggest mistakes of our lives.

If any of David's story rings true for you, I want to remind you that the same God who washed David's sins away is waiting for you. Our culture has done a pretty good job of shifting the lines between right and wrong: now anything goes. What our culture has not done, however, is provide an answer for the internal repercussions of abandoning God's ways. Anxiety, depression, and suicide are at epidemic rates. Now, let me say this, I don't believe that mental illness is caused by a sinful lifestyle. What I am saying is that when we're burdened with the scars of guilt from the choices we've made and don't know where to turn for help, anxiety and depression can be present or become greater. I know of a good man who killed himself because he couldn't bear to tell his wife that he had cheated on her and face the possibility of losing his children. I know of many who are addicted to online pornography—men and women who are afraid to confess their sin because it feels so dark. I understand that.

The church should be the place of greatest grace, but often it's where we're judged and thrown away. If you don't have a safe place right now, can I remind you that there is a safe Savior? No matter what you've done, there is no sin too great to separate you from the love of God (see Rom. 8:38–39), apart from denying who He is and rejecting the Holy Spirit. You don't have to clean yourself up; come as you are. The very things that make you feel disqualified from ever being used by God can be the channels through which He reaches another broken life. When wounds are fresh, they need space and grace to heal, but when scars begin to form, we have a story to share.

I read a Gallup poll recently talking about the fact that young people are leaving the church in droves. I wonder if part of that is because those of us who have walked through more of life don't share our scars? As long as we feel that we have to look perfect, we've missed the great opportunity to point someone else to Christ, who *is* perfect. I did a radio interview that allowed people to call in and ask questions. One woman asked, "Is it true that you ended up in a psych ward?" I assured her that it was. Then she asked, "Are you still on medication?" I assured her that I was. She said, "Then, I am so disappointed in you." I told her as kindly as I could that there was far more about me that would disappoint her. The one thing that was crystal clear to me that day in a small church in Washington, DC, was this:

I'm not the good news. Jesus is.

I wish I could sit down with you, look you in the eyes, and remind you that no matter what your scars are, internal or external, you are loved more than you have the capacity to bear. I think when we begin to grasp even the edges of that love it changes something deep inside. We want others to know it too. I titled this book *It's Okay Not to Be Okay.* I believe that. Christ meets us where we are. He doesn't leave us there, but that's where the journey begins. What's not okay is to pretend that you are okay when you know that you're not. Moving forward takes courage, but you will never walk one step of that journey by yourself. Christ is always with us.

Let me ask you something as I bring this chapter to a close: Are you willing to look at your scars? Some might be external ones that you've always seen as ugly. Christ doesn't. He welcomes you to bring your scars to Him. Talk to Him about them. Tell Him how you feel about them. Ask Him to touch them. Allow the love of God to rest upon your scars. Ask Him to help you see them not as scars to be hidden but as glorious tattoos of victory because you're still here! If your scars are internal because of choices you've made or things that have been done to you, don't let them be your identity anymore. Find your identity as a son or daughter of God. Christ wants to bring glory to the Father through your scars. When Jesus healed a blind man, His friends asked Him if the man or his parents had sinned to bring on this blindness. Jesus said no.

This happened so the power of God could be seen in him. (John 9:3)

Would you allow the power of God to be seen in you? He waits with outstretched nail-pierced hands.

One Step at a Time

Find Your Identity in Christ

1. There are many great quotes on scars, but for me this remains the simple truth: scars are proof that God heals and His love is greater than whatever tried to destroy us. Where are your scars? What are the things that have left their mark on you? Look—here you are! You made it! Will you take time to celebrate that what you thought would bring you down did not keep you down? Look how far you've come. Buy yourself a cupcake or a gluten-free muffin and rest in this moment for a while. Yes, there will be challenges ahead, but right now, take a deep breath and give thanks.

2. Your true identity is a gift from God. Becoming a Christian means you find out who you really are. You don't lose yourself when you become a Christian, you find out who you were always meant to be. Here's what God's Word says:

   God treasures you. *"God's very own possession."* 1 Peter 2:9

   He thinks you are worth dying for. *"For this is how God loved the world: He gave his one and only Son, so that everyone who believes in him will not perish but have eternal life."* John 3:16

   You are free! *"Now you are free from your slavery to sin, and you have become slaves to righteous living."* Romans 6:18

   You are forgiven. *"He is so rich in kindness and grace that he purchased our freedom with the blood of his Son and forgave our sins."* Ephesians 1:7

   Your eternal life is secure. *"I give them eternal life, and they will never perish. No one can snatch them away from me, for*

my Father has given them to me, and he is more powerful than anyone else. No one can snatch them from the Father's hand."
John 10:28–29

Choose one verse each day to meditate on. Write it on a sticky note and place it where you'll see it again and again.

eight

Decide to Start Again . . . and Again

And I am certain that God, who began the good work within you, will continue his work until it is finally finished on the day when Christ Jesus returns.

—Philippians 1:6

Once you are Real you can't be ugly, except to people who don't understand.

—Margery Williams, *The Velveteen Rabbit*

Have you ever watched someone you love do something a little crazy, spontaneous—something that seems out of character—only to realize that this actually is a piece of who they really are? Perhaps they're usually pretty quiet in a crowd and suddenly they become the life of the party, or you'd never put them in the category of a risk-taker and they suddenly step out and take the lead. I saw my husband do something like this last

Christmas. It was so unlike him that it made me laugh, but on reflection, I found it deeply touching. I saw that he'd reached a fresh place of freedom, a space where he felt comfortable enough in his own skin to let his goofy side show. He didn't just dip his toe in the water, however; he dove right in.

When Christian went back to college after Thanksgiving last year, I began to think about our family's Christmas. I wanted us to do something a little different. Christian is an only child, and we have no other family in America, so it means when he comes home for the holidays it's just us. There we are in all our glory: Barry, me, our three dogs, and, if Christian brings him home, Ramen the Danger Noodle, his pet snake. Even in matching Santa pajamas (the dogs as well—not the snake), we're a small tribe. I remember how much fun it was growing up with a brother and sister, and I've often wished that Christian had siblings too. I was forty years old when he was born, so we knew he might be an only child, but we prayed for more children. I did get pregnant one more time when Christian was two, but sadly, we lost that little one.

I decided that this year, especially since Christian's girlfriend was spending Christmas with us, we were going to have a fun, shake-it-up kind of holiday. I contemplated a skiing trip to the Rockies, but as I have the coordination and grace of a drunk moose I decided against that. Then I wondered about a trip to New York. There was a good chance of snow that Christmas, and the thought of sipping hot chocolate and watching the snow fall while being pulled along in a horse-drawn carriage was so appealing. I asked Barry and Christian what they thought. Christian was all in, but Barry had some concerns:

"What if there's another terrorist attack?"

"What if we get snowed in?"

"What if we get mugged?"

"What if we get snowed in with a mugger?"

I acknowledged to Eeyore that, yes, although remote, these were possibilities. Then I reminded him that, apart from the snowed-in bit, these could all happen in Dallas, so he agreed. I used my frequent-flyer miles for the flights and found a hotel right at the edge of Times Square. New York is a place that you either love or hate. Some people find the crowded streets and pace of life overwhelming, but I love it. The city feels so alive, and during the Christmas season, with the lights on Fifth Avenue and the magnificent tree in Rockefeller Center, it's a sparkling wonderland.

We had only four days, but we packed them with every fun thing we could imagine. We went ice skating in Rockefeller Center and watched a young man get down on one knee on the ice and ask his girlfriend to marry him. (She said yes!) We saw the Radio City Christmas Spectacular with the Rockettes and ate roasted chestnuts from a vendor roasting them right on the street. Barry and I took a cycle rickshaw back to the hotel and let Christian and his girlfriend take a horse-drawn-carriage ride through Central Park by themselves. At the top of my list was the quiet beauty of St. Patrick's Cathedral. Amid the noise and bustle of Fifth Avenue, packed with last-minute shoppers and honking cars and cabs, it was a gift to slip into the peace of this beautiful church and remember Christ, the true gift of Christmas.

On our last evening, as we walked the streets admiring the window displays and the Christmas lights, Barry . . . broke out. I don't know how else to put it. We were waiting to cross a very busy street, people were five or six layers deep, pushing against each other while waiting for the lights to change, and when they finally did, Barry took off. He began to hop across the street. I'm not talking about a little you-could-hardly-notice-it kind of hop—he went all "Elf" on us. I don't know what movies top your Christmas list each year, but in our family *Elf* sits right up there with *White Christmas* and *A Christmas Story*. One of our favorite scenes is when Buddy the Elf hops across a busy New York street, dodging yellow cabs at every turn. That was funny, but I have to say, Barry's hop was better. The street was heaving with people that night, but it didn't deter him a bit. I managed to pull out my iPhone in time, hit the video record button, and caught most of it. The thing that made it even more ridiculous is that nobody was paying any attention to this fifty-four-year-old man hopping like a gigantic Christmas bunny in the middle of Fifth Avenue. Clearly nothing fazes New Yorkers. They've seen it all. When we got back to our room that night I played it for him.

"What got into you?" I asked once we both stopped laughing.

"If you can't hop like a large bunny when you're fifty-four, when can you!" he said.

I love that! I wish that kind of freedom for you as well . . . not necessarily hopping like a giant bunny across a busy street, but the freedom to be all of who you really are. Most of us start off that way as children. When we're well loved it gives us space and grace to explore every area of our personality. We get to try things, we get to fall and fail and get back up again. When we're well loved we feel no shame in failing; it's accepted as part of the great adventure of life. We discover both what we love and are drawn to and the things that might be fun to try but clearly are not our strengths.

As we grow, however, life intrudes; other opinions are added to the mix, judgments are made, and we become less free. The school playground can be the first place to teach us that not everyone will welcome all of who we are. Perhaps your family laughed at all your little jokes as you were growing up so you assumed you were funny, but the feedback from this new crowd is cruel and unkind. Part of being well loved is getting honest, shame-free feedback as we grow. I thought I was really mastering the violin when I was a child until my family made it quite clear that if I continued they were pretty sure the cat was leaving home. We laughed about it together because there was no dismissive judgment, just honest feedback. So, I put the violin back into its case and apologized to the cat. Then my mum said, "But when you sing, Sheila, we all stop and listen."

A healthy family or friend can help us understand our strengths and weaknesses. The message is that not everything will work, but never be afraid to try and never be afraid to fail. Every failure takes us one step closer to where we'll shine. I had the privilege some time ago of interviewing one of America's most beloved Olympic skaters. He told me that he fell down over thirty thousand times, but he got back up over thirty thousand times. What a beautiful example of someone whose family taught him to persevere, knowing where his strength lay and refusing to let his dream die. There are, however, other reasons why dreams are abandoned and we lose who we really are.

Hiding the Real You

I was flipping through channels in a hotel room one night, looking for the local weather, when a woman's face on the screen made me stop. The camera had zoomed in on a tight shot of her face and the pain in her eyes was overwhelming. It looked to me as if she was trapped inside her own body, silently crying out for help. I sat down and watched the rest of the program. She weighed over 600 pounds, and the show was following her weight-loss journey. The camera moved from her face to pictures of her as a little girl. She was adorable, with curly blonde hair and sparkling blue eyes. The person who was interviewing her asked how old she was in those photos. She said she was six. Then the painful question came: "How did you get from that little girl to the way you are today?"

Her story poured out through tears. It was a story about sexual abuse when she was seven years old and the subsequent shame and self-loathing. Food had become the only friend she could trust. It brought her comfort and quiet when she was eating, but she knew that she was slowly killing herself. For her it was a death sentence. I watched the program for the full two hours, cheering her on when she succeeded and aching for her when she failed. She had gone from a bright, energetic child who loved to play soccer and ride her bike to a woman who hadn't been outside her home in over two years. As the program came to a close she had lost more than 300 pounds and was able to get up and walk in her neighborhood. The last shot was of her watching a girl riding her bike, and as I looked at this woman's face, I no longer saw the 300-pound woman: I saw that little girl with the blonde curls and the big blue eyes. She wasn't gone; she had just been hiding for a very long time.

Abuse or trauma in childhood impacts how much of the real you that you allow the world to see. You become more careful, more contained, because you've learned that life is not safe. Sexual abuse in particular brings with it an ocean of shame. One of my dearest friends was sexually abused by someone in her church when she was a little girl. That abuse triggered one of the most painful journeys I've ever seen. She became promiscuous as a teenager because, in her mind, sex equaled love and acceptance, but as she got older life became much more confusing. After she gave her life to Christ she was faced with this question: How could she love and trust God when her abuse was from someone who supposedly represented Him? It's taken a long time, intense counseling, and friends who won't give up on her to bring her to a place of peace and acceptance of the beautiful woman she is today. She had to fight hard to find herself again.

Finding Freedom

I travel around the country most weekends. I've never once been in a room of women, whether it was ten thousand or ten, where this issue has not been present. I've listened to those whose abuse drove them to meaningless sex with different partners and to those who are married and unable to have sex with their own husband because they equate it with what is wrong and dirty. In both situations, what should have been seen as a good gift from God has become a prison. Whenever I have an opportunity to sit down one-on-one with a woman who has experienced this trauma, I listen to her story for as long as it takes. Then I remind her of the description of Christ, first from the prophet Isaiah (Isa. 61:1–2) and then from Christ's own lips:

> The Spirit of the LORD is upon me,
>> for he has anointed me to bring Good News to the poor.
> He has sent me to proclaim that captives will be released,
>> that the blind will see,
> that the oppressed will be set free,
>> and that the time of the LORD's favor has come. (Luke
>> 4:18–19)

Christ was anointed to free those who are in prison and those who can barely lift their heads from the weight of shame. It began so long ago. Shame was introduced in the Garden of Eden (Gen. 3). Then Christ, the second Adam, came to take our shame upon Himself. Every one of us is invited to begin that journey from the place where we were shamed to the place where we begin to experience the freedom Christ offers. I love what I read in a blog recently:

> There is nothing that robs the perpetrator of haunting our memories or possessing our soul like our identification with the passion of Christ. We are so much more than what has happened to us. We need to reorient our whole identity with His life in us. We have to finish the journey going from the garden to the cross, from being overwhelmed at the garden to being victorious at the cross, defeating death and shame forever. Not that we would be rid of our pain . . . not necessarily . . . but that the pain would be redeemed pain.[1]

Redeemed pain. That's a powerful truth. We all experience pain, but when we bring it to Jesus, He redeems it. The enemy of our soul would love to keep us quiet and shame-filled, but Jesus uses pain given to Him to free us and to see others set free. You are not what happened to you. You are a child of God.

You are not *what happened* to you. You are a *child of God.*

Not all abuse is sexual. Some is verbal or physical. Verbal abuse chips away at your very soul. Whoever coined the phrase "Sticks and stones may break my bones, but words will never hurt me" had likely never been hurt. I found a reference to that saying in a magazine from 1862 (in *The Christian Recorder*, March 1862). In that magazine it was referred to as "an old adage," so it's clearly been around for a long time. It may be familiar but it's not true. Words hurt. Words can wound and tear down. Words can become labels that we wear around our neck, believing this is who we are. I asked a small group of women recently to talk about the labels they wear. They were quiet for a while, so I waited. Then, as they spoke, I understood their reticence to share.

Divorced

Single mother

Fat

Ugly

Old

Adulterer

Unwanted

Crazy

These beautiful women had allowed the cruel, thoughtless words of someone else to construct a prison in which they now lived. Labels can inform us or they can confine us. We all walk through difficult times, and I don't know a single person who, when looking back on their lives, imagined things would unfold the way they did. But as the blog piece said, you are not what happened to you. When you allow a label to become the greatest truth about yourself, you've missed out on the glorious redemption Christ bought for you on the cross.

Redemption sounds like a word for ancient times, but its meaning is powerful. Imagine that you had committed a crime and a price of ten million dollars was being asked for bail to be granted. Impossible. Very few of us could ever come up with that kind of money. What Christ did was far greater than pay our bond. Not only did He cover our bond, He took our place for the crime. From a hopeless situation the prison doors were thrown open and we were told we're free. When you have placed your trust in Christ, that is the label that defines you—child of God. Yes, we might be divorced or overweight, we might struggle with mental illness or be scarred on our faces, but none of these things define us. Rather, like my brave friend who sat through a woman's conference, the very things that we think would disqualify us become the places that remind us daily of the grace of God.

As I looked into the eyes of these darling women, I asked them to write those labels that had previously defined them on a piece of paper and roll it up tight. Then I gave each one a biodegradable paper lantern (we don't want to harm the planet) and asked her to tape the paper into the inside of the lantern. I did it too. I prayed over each woman and lifted her to Christ, asking that He teach us all who we really are. Then we went outside and lit the tiny flames inside each lantern that would take them to the sky, and we let them go. As they soared over the trees and rooftops, I read some Scripture verses I'd prepared for that day.

> The LORD your God is in your midst;
>   a mighty one who will save;
> he will rejoice over you with gladness;
>   he will quiet you by his love;
> he will exult over you with loud singing. (Zeph. 3:17 ESV)

> Can a mother forget her nursing child?
>   Can she feel no love for the child she has borne?
> But even if that were possible,
>   I would not forget you! (Isa. 49:15)

When you allow a label

to become the greatest

truth about yourself,

you've missed out on the

glorious *redemption*

Christ bought for you

on the cross.

So we have stopped evaluating others from a human point of view. At one time we thought of Christ merely from a human point of view. How differently we know him now! This means that anyone who belongs to Christ has become a new person. The old life is gone; a new life has begun! (2 Cor. 5:16–17)

I knew it would take more than a simple balloon release to eradicate the messages that had become so ingrained in all of us, but it was a start. As I've worked on and prayed over this book, it has become crystal clear to me that the way we move forward isn't with a giant leap, it's one step at a time. We want the leap, we want everything to change in big ways that are recognizable and significant, but lasting progress doesn't usually happen that way. Not only that, when we wait for the big leap we can miss the progress that takes place little by little every single day with each simple step. I remember a friend telling me about one of her trips. She is an avid photographer, and every day she stood on the deck of the ship waiting to spot a whale. One morning, she noticed a little penguin doing a funny dance on a sheet of ice. She said, "All this time I've been waiting for a whale and this little guy was saying, 'Don't miss me!'"

Don't miss the simple steps. Don't think that they don't matter. For me, taking one step at a time has become a daily act of worship. It's aligning my heart and mind with who God says I am. I would love to say that at this stage in my life I have arrived, but I am still very much on this journey with you.

Understanding the Real You

Do you ever wonder why you respond a certain way when you find yourself in a particular situation? You might get angry about things that don't seem worthy of your anger and you wonder where it's coming from, or a line in a movie or a song strikes something deep inside and you find yourself very emotional. For me this overreaction has happened with my husband, and it was very hard and confusing to both of us until I began to understand where it all began. It began when I was five.

It's hard to believe that what happened to me as a five-year-old could still cast its shadow so many years later, but it does. How it manifests itself is that in certain circumstances, I become unreasonably afraid. Barry would ask me to explain why I was afraid so he could understand. The problem was that I didn't understand it myself.

This fear showed up most often while Barry and I were in the car together. I know that in most marriages, jokes are made about each other's driving. It wasn't a joke for me, and because of that, not for Barry either. Let me say this upfront: Barry is a really good driver. He's not reckless or distracted. Despite that, my stomach would be in knots when he was driving. I would grab my seat or make noises as if I was bracing for a crash. As you can imagine, it drove him crazy. Many times he would ask me to drive, just to get peace. It really bothered me because I knew my reaction hurt him, but I seemed to have no control over it. Then he began to notice something. If we were out of town and being driven by our hosts, I was never nervous. It's hard for a husband not to take that personally! I began to ask God to help me understand why I responded that way. Why couldn't I trust the one person who is committed to loving me for life?

The answer was surprising. The fact that Barry is the one person I trust most in this world was exactly the issue. The one I trusted most in the world before him was my dad. Even though as an adult I understood that it was a brain injury that caused my dad's rage against me, my last encounter with him was life-or-death. I have no doubt that had he been able to bring his cane down on my skull, he would have killed me. I stopped him by making him lose his balance. Clearly as a child I had internalized the message that the one you love most is potentially the most dangerous. After all these years, two seminaries, and twenty years of speaking at women's conferences, I still hadn't connected the way I reacted to my loving husband with the pain of my past. I'd love to say that once I understood that I was all better, but it's a journey I'm still on.

A couple of weeks ago, Barry came into our bedroom where I was folding laundry, and he held out my phone, which I'd left in the kitchen. In his mind he was going to do something cute. Rather than give me my phone he planned to grab my hand and pull me to him. It didn't go well. He honestly scared me. My heart was beating out of my chest as I sat on the bed and cried like a little girl, because that's who was crying.

My family's way of coping was to pretend that nothing had happened. We never talked about my dad, never mentioned his name. Although I still experience moments like that, understanding why I react the way I do has helped me bring that broken piece of myself into the healing light of Christ's presence. Now, I talk to Jesus about it. I have had to bring the little girl in me to Jesus over and over and ask Him to help her. That may sound a little strange to you, but we serve the God who was there in all our yesterdays, is here with us today, and will be with us in all our tomorrows. He invites us to bring to Him all of who we were, who we are, and who we hope to be. If you have been impacted by abuse in your past, find a photograph of yourself at that age (if you have one) and let that younger you know that Jesus has got her back and so do you. You might want to remind her of this amazing truth:

> You made all the delicate, inner parts of my body
>> and knit me together in my mother's womb.
> Thank you for making me so wonderfully complex!
>> Your workmanship is marvelous—how well I know it.
> You watched me as I was being formed in utter seclusion,
>> as I was woven together in the dark of the womb.
> You saw me before I was born.
>> Every day of my life was recorded in your book.
> Every moment was laid out
>> before a single day had passed.

How precious are your thoughts about me, O God.
>   They cannot be numbered!
I can't even count them;
>   they outnumber the grains of sand!
And when I wake up,
>   you are still with me! (Ps. 139:13–18)

Loving the Broken You

It's a little unusual to see one lone male face at a woman's event, but there he was, ten rows from the front. I wondered if his wife had played a joke on him and told him it was a men's conference and now he was boxed in by a bevy of beauties? I signed books and talked to women for about an hour after the event, and I saw that he was waiting to talk to me, the right side of his face turned into the wall. When the last woman had gone, he walked over to me and introduced himself and his daughter who was with him.

He touched the right side of his face, which was badly scarred, and told me in a faint, scratchy voice that when he was fifteen he had tried to kill himself. He put a loaded gun under his chin and fired. He said that in the millisecond between pulling the trigger and the bullet entering his skull he heard Christ ask him if he wanted to live. He said yes.

He was now in his forties with six children, one of them the beautiful young girl who was by his side. I was overwhelmed by his story. I've sat and wept with families when a loved one has taken their own life but never with one who seriously meant to die and lived to tell their story. He told me that the bullet is still in his skull as it would be too dangerous to remove and that his voice is permanently damaged. I asked him if that was a harsh reminder of his past. He told me that it was the absolute opposite. He said that he has a daily reminder of the grace and mercy of God. He has learned to love the brokenness in himself and offer it to Christ. He plans to start an outreach to young people who might be in the same place he was when he was fifteen years old.

The truth about our lives is that we are all broken. It's more obvious when the scar is on the skin and not on the soul, but we are broken nonetheless. The decision we get to make is whether we hide that brokenness or offer it to Jesus.

I've always loved the Velveteen Rabbit story. I loved it before I knew why I loved it. I now know that there was something I longed for in the idea that once you become *real* you can never be ugly except to those who don't understand. I wanted to be real, but I was afraid that the real me was ugly and disappointing. To Jesus, we are never ugly or disappointing; we are loved.

The reason I loved Barry's Elf hop across the street, other than the glorious spectacle of it all, is that he wouldn't have been able to do that a few years ago. He was teased and bullied at school because he was shorter than the other boys in his grade. He did hit a growth spurt when he was in college, but by then the mean messages had been scratched into his soul. He didn't want to stand out; he tried to blend in. Adding to that, his mom and dad were overprotective and taught him that the world is not safe. In the first few years of our marriage Barry hid his panic attacks from me. He was ashamed of feeling so out of control. Then, when he was able to let me in and help me understand, he didn't want Christian to know. I think it's harder for a guy to admit to something that feels weak than it is for a woman. Interestingly, in recent months the things we tried to shield our son from have been the very things that have brought us closer as a family.

One evening when Christian was home from college, he was sharing with us about some of his friends who are really struggling with depression and anxiety but were afraid to let their parents know in case they didn't understand. I felt so convicted about trying to cover the areas where I need Christ's help most from our son. How was I helping him know where to show up when he needed help? That night Barry and I both shared the real us to our son. He received it as if we had given him a gift. I suppose we did. Christ is the only one who makes us all *real*.

As Barry and I have grown together, the greatest healing has occurred by being able to bring all of who we are to each other and to Christ. We've told each other the worst we've ever been told about ourselves, the worst we've believed, and we've learned to laugh at ourselves, together. As I watched him leap across a crowded New York street, I laughed, not just because it was goofy but because Barry was comfortable enough in his own skin to break out all the goofy that was in him. At this stage in life we both get that we'll never be perfect, we'll never be everything each other might have wanted in a spouse, and that's okay. It's more than okay, it's a gift. When you realize that you don't have to have it all together you can give others that freedom too. Understanding that Christ is the hero of our stories allows us to be human.

One of the verses that has become a life verse for both of us is the one at the beginning of this chapter:

> And I am certain that God, who began the good work within you, will continue his work until it is finally finished on the day when Christ Jesus returns. (Phil. 1:6)

Understanding that God is the one who will get us all home makes it possible to enjoy the journey.

Trusting the Real God to Complete the Work in the Real You

When I was sixteen, I volunteered at a retirement home two nights a week and on Saturdays. My responsibilities were fairly basic. I changed bed linens, cleaned bathrooms, and made tea. I loved it and became very fond of several of the residents. I found it sad that

Understanding that Christ is the *hero* of our stories allows us to be *human*.

some of them never had a visitor, so I signed my mum and my sister up as visitors!

One night a nurse had given me a bowl of soup to take to a resident who'd been asleep during dinner. As I left the nurses' station I realized that she hadn't given me a spoon, so I headed back to the kitchen to get one. As I passed the nurses' station I overheard this comment: "I don't know what we're going to do next week. Two of the nurses are sick and one's on vacation. Who's going to run this place?"

I didn't think much about that as I had to get "Fred" a spoon, so I popped into the kitchen and picked one up. As I passed their station on the way back, I heard, "Don't worry, Sheila's got it. She can do this by herself now."

I totally panicked. I gave "Fred" his soup and headed back to their office. I knocked tentatively on the door, and when I was invited to come in I blurted out, "I'm so sorry. I love volunteering here, I really do. But I can't do it all by myself. I'm only sixteen!"

With that, I burst into tears. Well, as you can imagine, I'd overheard parts of two conversations. I'd actually been entrusted with giving "Fred" his soup, not the running of the entire home. It was quite a relief.

Sometimes we live as if the whole responsibility of living this Christian journey is all up to us, and it's overwhelming. We see what's broken and where we fall short and think we'll never make it all the way home. When Paul wrote to the church in Philippi he reminded them, and us, that it was God who began the work. Not only that, he reminded them that God will continue it until the day when we are finally home with Christ.

It's helpful to note that when Paul wrote this letter he was a prisoner living under the shadow of possible execution. He's not writing it from a lounge chair at the edge of the ocean; he's in shackles, and yet the message remains: God's got this. The word that Paul uses for *certain* is the Greek word *peitho*, the strongest word he could have used to describe his absolute conviction about what he was about to share. All of Scripture makes one thing clear: when God begins something He already has the end in sight. If you're like me, you've started projects you never finished, but God never has. He is the Alpha and Omega, the beginning and the end. We are safe in His care. When Jesus described Himself as the Good Shepherd, He made it clear that no one takes us away from Him:

> My sheep listen to my voice; I know them, and they follow me. I give them eternal life, and they will never perish. No one can snatch them away from me, for my Father has given them to me, and he is more powerful than anyone else. No one can snatch them from the Father's hand. The Father and I are one. (John 10:27–30)

I have shelves of Bible commentaries at home, and one of my favorite series is *Black's New Testament Commentaries*. Marcus Bockmuehl wrote the commentary on Paul's letter to the Philippians, and I love how he unpacks the truth of Philippians 1:6:

> In all this, Paul's confidence is not in the Christianity of the Christians but in the God-ness of God, who is supremely trustworthy, able, and committed to finish the work he has begun.[2]

Don't you love that? Our confidence is not based on whether you or I are doing a good job but rather in God, our Father, who is faithful to finish what He began. You can rest in that. You can take that to the bank. When you are fed up with yourself and feel as if you'll never make real progress, remind yourself, it's not up to me, it's up to my Father—and He never fails.

Augustus Toplady summed up this great truth in his hymn "A Debtor to Mercy Alone":

> The work which His goodness began,
> The arm of His strength will complete;

When you are fed up with yourself and feel as if you'll never make real *progress*, remind yourself, it's not up to me, it's up to my Father— and He *never fails*.

His promise is Yea and Amen,
And never was forfeited yet.

Take One More Step

I'm sitting at my dining room table in our home in Dallas. Barry and I just took our three dogs for a walk, and halfway home the skies opened up and poured down with rain, so he's upstairs attempting to dry three very cross dogs. I'm sitting here thinking about you and praying for you. I don't know the hard things that happened in your life and made you hide. I don't know what labels you've worn or how deeply ingrained those messages are. What I'm asking God is simply this:

Father,

Would You give her (or him) the grace to bring those labels to You? Would You help them take a long, hard look at what they have believed about themselves, but then, would You help them see themselves as You do—loved, known, accepted? We know that we're not okay, but because of what You have done for us, we are more than okay: we are redeemed. Help us each day to take one more step toward everything that is true and one step further away from the lies we have believed. Help us take one more step, every day, closer to You.

In Christ's name,

Amen

One Step at a Time

Move Forward Every Single Day

1. "This means that anyone who belongs to Christ has become a new person. The old life is gone; a new life has begun!" (2 Cor. 5:17)

   I love the word *begin*. It speaks to something new, moving forward, taking the next step. Plant joy in your heart. You get to start again . . . and again . . . and again.

   Now, let's deal with the labels you've worn. How do you believe others see you? Are you

   a single mom?

   a divorced dad?

   one who had an affair?

   an alcoholic?

   fat?

   rejected?

   a financial failure?

   in a mess?

   a Sunday-only Christian?

   an "it's all about me" friend?

   Whatever labels you have worn until this point, are you willing to let them go? Are you ready to identify yourself in Christ? Declare these truths over your life:

   I am an overcomer.

   I can do all things through Christ who gives me strength.

I am part of heaven's royal family.

I am a new creation.

I have a future and a hope.

Just as I am, right now, I am completely loved by God.

2. Do you realize that before you were even born God knew and loved you? This is what David writes:

> You made all the delicate, inner parts of my body
> and knit me together in my mother's womb.
> Thank you for making me so wonderfully complex!
> Your workmanship is marvelous—how well I know it.
> You watched me as I was being formed in utter seclusion,
> as I was woven together in the dark of the womb.
> You saw me before I was born.
> Every day of my life was recorded in your book.
> Every moment was laid out
> before a single day had passed.
>
> How precious are your thoughts about me, O God.
> They cannot be numbered!
> I can't even count them;
> they outnumber the grains of sand!
> And when I wake up,
> you are still with me! (Ps. 139:13–18)

Meditate on these verses. Every single day of your life before you took your first breath, God knew and loved you. Find the youngest photo of yourself you can find. If you don't have baby photos then write down in your journal the day you were born and then write beside it, "I was known and loved before this."

The great hope for moving forward is this: If you have a pulse, as long as there's not a white chalk mark around your body, it's never too late to start again . . . and again.

Conclusion

You Were Made for More

But my life is worth nothing to me unless I use it for finishing the work assigned me by the Lord Jesus—the work of telling others the Good News about the wonderful grace of God.

—Acts 20:24

"Go back?" he thought. "No good at all! Go sideways? Impossible! Go forward? Only thing to do! On we go!"

—J. R. R. Tolkien, *The Hobbit*

In Scotland all the high schools in each town gathered together every spring for Sports Day. It was a very big deal. All the parents would come and sit in the stands, and at the end of the day, our town mayor would present medals and a challenge cup to the winning school and individual athletes. Unfortunately, participation, in my school, was not optional.

I am not an athletic person. I consider a brief jog to the coffeepot in the morning worthy of some kind of recognition. As a teenager I couldn't find any sport where I could shine, but the most challenging thing of all was track. Running seemed unnecessary to me unless I was about to miss a bus.

Our school was divided into four houses, each given a different color. I was blue, and it mirrored my feelings every single Sports Day. All students were required to compete in at least one of the track races. The 200 meters was a fast run, and you had to be able to take off like a bullet and maintain that pace until you crossed the finish line. I had no bullet in me. The relay race needed the four strongest runners, so I was out for that one too. The 2,000 meters called for stamina, which I was a little short on, so every year my team put me up for the 500-meter race. You didn't have to be super fast or maintain much endurance; you just had to start, keep going, and finish. I did it every year. I started, kept going, and finished last. It would have been nice if one year I'd finished second to last, but it was not meant to be. Even so, my mum faithfully cheered for me as I hobbled over the finish line. My teammates were less effusive. "Stick to singing!" I was told.

Barry doesn't fall into the athletic category either, which is why it was surprising to both of us to discover that our son does. He played football and soccer in high school and now, in college, is a certified scuba diver and a very competent skier.

On our very first family ski trip Barry and I learned an important lesson. There are times in life when the only place to go is forward, even if everything within you is screaming to go back. I'd watched skiing on television and it looked easy. All you had to do was point those things downhill and off you went. Not only that, the clothes are so cute. So, when Christian was ten we headed to Colorado for spring break. As it was the first time on the slopes for all of us, we signed up for a lesson. Christian picked it up immediately. He seemed fearless and was cleared by the instructor to join some of his school friends, who were also vacationing there, on the first level of green runs.

I found the beginner bunny hill a bit challenging. The instructor kept telling me to make like a pizza slice with my skis, but mine were more like a pizza roll. I decided that I was struggling because the hill was too shallow. After all, the people I watched in the Winter Olympics headed downhill, not side to side. Barry agreed. The bunny slope was not for us; we were made for more. At the end of our lesson the instructor suggested we sign up for another lesson the following day and the day after that. We thanked him and told him, "We've got this." We were ready. It was time for the big leagues.

We got in line for the Drink of Water Chairlift full of confident hope that soon we would be zipping downhill, me in my pink-and-white outfit and Barry, all American, in red, white, and blue.

Getting on a chairlift is a bit challenging. It doesn't stop to let you board, which seemed poorly thought-out to me. You have to catch it as it comes up behind you, sit, pull down the bar, and hold on. Well, we managed that. The scenery on the way up was breathtaking. It was still early in the day and many of the slopes were untouched. The snow sparkled like diamonds in the sun. Barry had his eyes closed the whole time. I thought he was praying but discovered later he's afraid of heights. That should have been a clue right there.

"Wouldn't it be amazing if we are really good at this?" I said, gazing at a lone skier gracefully making his way down the mountain beneath us.

"It would!" he agreed, eyes still shut. "If we'd worked this out earlier in life who knows where we'd be now."

I now know. We'd be in a full body cast.

If I thought getting *on* the chairlift was challenging, nothing had prepared me for getting *off*. I watched the people ahead of us as they reached the top.

"We just ski off!" I said to Barry. "You'll have to open your eyes! They don't give you much time."

The minute I put my skis on the snow and the chair moved on, I fell flat on my face, which made disembarking challenging for the couple behind us. They fell on top of me as I tried to crawl away.

They got right back up and skied off, muttering something about "rookie skiers" under their breath. Barry didn't fall but he didn't stop either. He skied head-first into a trash can and then landed on his rear end. I crawled over to him, one ski on and one ski off. It wasn't the most promising start.

"Shake it off. We've got this," I said. "No one tells you how to get on and off that blooming thing. Skiing will be a lot easier."

We each posed for a couple of photographs, poles in hand, ski glasses on, looking very . . . Olympic. With both skis back on, I joined Barry to look at the sign telling us which runs were available from this point on the mountain. Some were marked blue and looked more difficult. We decided that, although we could probably manage them, we'd start with a green run. We settled for one called Red Buffalo. I liked the sound of that. As the buffalo races across the plain, we too would begin this race we were born for.

We stood at the top of the run for a moment looking down. It was quite steep. Even so, large groups of children were taking off effortlessly down the hill and they didn't even have poles. So, I took a deep breath, smiled at Barry, and tipped my skis downhill.

I discovered that I did have a bullet in me after all! I took off at such a ridiculous speed, straight downhill, and realized that I'd never asked where the brakes were. (Yes, I do know now that there are no brakes.) So I did the only thing I could think of, I fell over. I landed hard on the snow, my glasses went one way and one ski and my poles another. I heard a little girl screaming so I turned around and realized that it was Barry. He was heading right for me. From the look of absolute horror on his face it was clear that his first run wasn't going any better than mine. I braced for the hit. He banged into me then rolled a little further down the hill. I took off my remaining ski and crawled down to see if he was still alive.

"What were we thinking!" he said, once he'd caught his breath. "We can't do this. We're not skiers. We like the lazy river."

"Wait there," I said. "I have to get my stuff back."

I left the ski I had with him and crawled back up the hill, dodging angry skiers all the way. I found my remaining ski and my poles, but my glasses were gone. Either someone had picked them up or they were now buried deep in the snow. I wrote them off as collateral damage and crawled back down to where Barry was now lying flat on his back.

"What are we going to do?" I said. "We're halfway down the mountain. We can't crawl all the way back up. We have to get down."

"Is there a bus?" he asked.

"Barry, we're on a mountain, not at a mall. We have to get down."

"What about a rescue team?" he suggested.

"That's for people who're hurt, not for people who're stupid!"

Now, I realize that if you are a skier this sounds ridiculous, but we were genuinely terrified. It was a long way down, and the misplaced confidence we had at the top had left with my glasses.

"We'll just stay here then," he said. "Christian will have them send out a search party if we don't return."

"You want a ten-year-old boy to have to get help because his mom and dad are stuck halfway down a beginner hill?" I asked. "No way. We've got to do this. We have to put our skis back on and help each other down the mountain."

It's hard putting skis on when you're on a hill, but finally we got them on and slowly, I mean slowly, going from side to side across the hill we finally made our way to the bottom. When we caught up with Christian, his friends, and their parents later in the day, he was glowing.

"Wasn't that amazing!" he said.

"Yep . . . we're both amazed," I said.

"That we're still alive," Barry muttered under his breath.

We were fortunate to leave that trip with nothing more than a few scrapes and bruised egos, but I took something with me from that experience that has proved to be true over and over again. There are moments, even seasons in life, when you have to set yourself in one direction and fight, no matter how hard it is, to make it through. I find this to be true in my walk with Christ. It's easy to believe and take the next step when things are going well, but when you find yourself stuck between who you used to be and who you want to be in Christ, it can be a spiritual battle. Think of Peter stepping out of the boat onto the rough sea. Perhaps, like me, he thought, "I've got this," but the lesson he learned that night taught him more about Christ's enough-ness and not his own.

> About three o'clock in the morning Jesus came toward them, walking on the water. When the disciples saw him walking on the water, they were terrified. In their fear, they cried out, "It's a ghost!"
>
> But Jesus spoke to them at once. "Don't be afraid," he said. "Take courage. I am here!"
>
> Then Peter called to him, "Lord, if it's really you, tell me to come to you, walking on the water."
>
> "Yes, come," Jesus said.
>
> So Peter went over the side of the boat and walked on the water toward Jesus. But when he saw the strong wind and the waves, he was terrified and began to sink. "Save me, Lord!" he shouted.
>
> Jesus immediately reached out and grabbed him. "You have so little faith," Jesus said. "Why did you doubt me?"
>
> When they climbed back into the boat, the wind stopped. Then the disciples worshiped him. "You really are the Son of God!" they exclaimed. (Matt. 14:25–33)

Peter had to constantly battle with who he knew himself to be and who he longed to be as a disciple of Christ. We're familiar with the night that he betrayed Christ, but it's easy to miss what Jesus told him just a few hours before that. In the NKJV it reads like this:

> And the Lord said, "Simon, Simon! Indeed, Satan has asked for you, that he may sift you as wheat. But I have prayed for you, that your

faith should not fail; and when you have returned to Me, strengthen your brethren." (Luke 22:31–32)

In the original language it's made clear that Satan had asked to sift the disciples, plural, but that Christ had prayed for Peter, singular, as reflected here:

Simon, Simon, Satan has asked to sift each of you like wheat. But I have pleaded in prayer for you, Simon, that your faith should not fail. So when you have repented and turned to me again, strengthen your brothers.(Luke 22:31–32)

In essence Christ was telling Peter, "You're going to have to fight for your faith. It's not going to be easy, but when you repent and turn around, help your brothers become stronger."

I love that after the resurrection Christ asked Peter three times if he loved Him. Three times he had denied even knowing Christ, but on the beach that morning he was given an opportunity to publicly declare his love three times.

After breakfast Jesus asked Simon Peter, "Simon son of John, do you love me more than these?"

"Yes, Lord," Peter replied, "you know I love you."

"Then feed my lambs," Jesus told him.

Jesus repeated the question: "Simon son of John, do you love me?"

"Yes, Lord," Peter said, "you know I love you."

"Then take care of my sheep," Jesus said.

A third time he asked him, "Simon son of John, do you love me?"

Peter was hurt that Jesus asked the question a third time. He said, "Lord, you know everything. You know that I love you."

Jesus said, "Then feed my sheep." (John 21:15–17)

Some commentaries suggest that the only reason Jesus asked Peter three times if he loved Him was to cancel out the three denials, but

I think there's more. I think Christ was testing where Peter was in his faith. Was he still the same brash, self-confident fisherman who vowed he'd never fail, or was he now a man who knew where his strength lay: in Christ alone?

When Jesus asks Peter "do you love me" the first two times, He uses the word *agapaō*. This is the word we get *agape* love from, signifying the divine love between God and us. Peter replies with the weaker form of that word, *phileō*, a word describing brotherly love between friends. The third time Christ uses Peter's word, *phileō*, and Peter, grieved, answers that yes, he loves Jesus with a flawed human love. From that place of transparent vulnerability Christ commissions Peter to be the one to feed His sheep. It was significant that He did that in front of the other disciples. They knew how Peter had failed. They knew the shock and agony of Christ being crucified and how he wept bitterly at leaving Jesus when He needed Peter most. Now Christ was saying to all that Peter would be the one to lead. He goes on to let Peter know a little of what was ahead for him.

> I tell you the truth, when you were young, you were able to do as you liked; you dressed yourself and went wherever you wanted to go. But when you are old, you will stretch out your hands, and others will dress you and take you where you don't want to go. (John 21:18)

As a young man Peter had been able to do what he wanted with his life, but now, in humble, sold-out service to Jesus he would be taken where he would never have chosen to go. Church history records for us that indeed Peter was taken out and crucified, but the man who said he didn't know Jesus no longer lived: he had been transformed. As his arms were being stretched out to be nailed to his cross Peter asked to be crucified upside down, as he thought he wasn't worthy to die the same death as his Lord and Savior. Peter lost confidence in himself and instead was filled with faith in the risen Christ.

More

I began this book with the very basic truth that it's okay not to be okay. Jesus knows us and loves us as we are whether we feel weak or strong. But I want to finish by encouraging you to fight for more. Every person I encounter in Scripture who was willing to wrestle with their faith, to fight to know more of God, was changed. Think of Job. We looked at some of his story. We looked at how he wrestled with God in the midst of his pain. He didn't "play nice"—he fought hard. God commended him for refusing to be quiet. He brought all of his complaints to God, and in the end, Job said this:

> I had only heard about you before,
>> but now I have seen you with my own eyes. (Job 42:5)

That statement challenged me for years. The implication was crystal clear: Will you fight for a faith that is your own or settle for what everyone tells you about God? In my darkest days, on the floor of my hospital room in a psych ward, I chose to fight. Like Peter, I was grieved by my own failures. As a teenager I used to walk along the shoreline where I lived in Scotland and declare to God that even if everyone else failed Him, I never would. Now, I had been taken to a place where I would never have signed up to go, but it was there as I wept in the ashes of my own failure that I could say with Job, "I had only heard about you before, but now I have seen you with my own eyes."

I had been a Christian at that point for twenty-five years. I'd been trained for ministry in seminary. I'd sat on the set of a national television show every day for five years and talked about the love of God, but I was still living in a prison of shame and fear. God in His mercy took me to a prison to set me free. When there was absolutely nothing left to commend me, Jesus asked me, "Sheila, do you love Me?" On the floor of that room I said, "Yes." But, it wasn't the yes of "I've got this." It was the tear-soaked yes of finally understanding that I'll never be enough. I'll never be okay, but that wasn't what He was asking me. He was asking, "Do you love Me?" Measuring our lives and our service to Christ by whether we're okay or not is a soul-destroying way to live. We will always be two steps forward and three steps back. Here's the shift: Christ asks, "Do you love Me?"

Our behavior too often holds us back because we get discouraged by our own failures. That's not how Christ sees or values you and me. Instead He simply asks if we love Him. Rules attempt to modify our behavior, but love, the love of God, changes our hearts. When our hearts are free to love with abandon, knowing that we're not being judged for every failure, our behavior changes. It changes not because we have to, but because we love Him so much that we want to. The love of Christ propels us to take the next step, and the next, and the next. It's never been about being better behaved; it's always been about us being more in love—and nothing, nothing, *nothing* can ever separate us from that love.

> And I am convinced that nothing can ever separate us from God's love. Neither death nor life, neither angels nor demons, neither our fears for today nor our worries about tomorrow—not even the powers of hell can separate us from God's love. No power in the sky above or in the earth below—indeed, nothing in all creation will ever be able to separate us from the love of God that is revealed in Christ Jesus our Lord. (Rom. 8:38–39)

What's Next

Thank you for taking this journey with me. I'm proud of you! Some steps may have been easier to take than others, but I think the ones that are the most difficult contain the greatest reward.

When our *hearts* are free

to love with abandon,

knowing that we're not being

judged for every failure,

our behavior *changes*.

You are worth fighting for.

Your faith is worth fighting for.

Christ is worth fighting for.

Some steps in this book you'll have to go back to over and over again. But that's okay, because when you take one step at a time, you're moving forward every single day. When you place your hand in the hand of Christ and say "Yes!" to the little steps and the big steps you will never be the same again. It's the greatest adventure in life!

And I am certain that God, who began the good work within you, will continue his work until it is finally finished on the day when Christ Jesus returns. (Phil. 1:6)

Acknowledgments

Thank you first to Baker Publishing Group. This is my first book with Baker Books, and I am so happy to be part of the family. You have such a rich heritage and commitment to building up the body of Christ through books that are relevant, intelligent, and engaging. It's an honor to publish with you.

I am profoundly grateful to my editor, Rebekah Guzman. It was a joy not only to work with you but to become your friend. Thank you for your hard work and invaluable insight.

And to Mark Rice, Eileen Hanson, Dave Lewis, and everyone else who had a part in this book at Baker, thank you for believing in this message.

To James and Betty Robison, thank you for the privilege of working side by side with you through Life Outreach International, bringing hope and healing to a broken world.

And to my son, Christian. You are a constant source of love and encouragement. I love being your mum.

Finally, to my husband, Barry. You have walked and prayed with me through every page of this book. I am so grateful and I love you.

Jesus—you make every day worth living.

Notes

Chapter 2 Admit That You Are Stuck and Struggling

1. Shauna Niequist, *Bittersweet* (Grand Rapids: Zondervan, 2013), 94.

Chapter 3 Change the Way You Think

1. Rick Warren, http://pastorrick.com/devotional/english/full-post/to-change
-how-you-act-change-the-way-you-think.

Chapter 4 Face the What-Ifs Even If You Are Afraid

1. R. V. G. Tasker, *The Gospel According to St. Matthew*, Tyndale Bible Commentaries, vol. 1 (Grand Rapids: Eerdmans, 1961), 168.

2. R. T. France, in William MacDonald, *Believer's Bible Commentary* (Nashville:
Thomas Nelson, 1995), 266.

3. Jim Elliot quote, http://www2.wheaton.edu/bgc/archives/faq/20.htm.

4. Warren Wiersbe, *The Wiersbe Bible Commentary, Old Testament* (Colorado
Springs: David C. Cook, 2007), 661.

Chapter 5 Let Go of What You Can't Control

1. University of Rochester Medical Center Health Encyclopedia, https://www
.urmc.rochester.edu/encyclopedia/content.aspx?ContentTypeID=1&ContentID
=3051.

Chapter 6 Rise above Disappointment

1. Charles Spurgeon quote, https://www.goodreads.com/quotes/1403154-god
-is-too-good-to-be-unkind-and-he-is.

Chapter 7 Celebrate Your Scars as Tattoos of Triumph

1. Augustus M. Toplady, "Rock of Ages," public domain.

2. C. H. Spurgeon, from a sermon delivered on Sabbath evening, January 30, 1859, at New Park Street Chapel, Southwark, http://www.romans45.org/spurgeon/sermons/0254.htm.

Chapter 8 Decide to Start Again . . . and Again

1. Biblical Soul Care Harvest Bible Chapel, "Victory over the Shame of Sexual Abuse," *Association of Biblical Counselors* (blog), Biblestudytools.com, https://www.biblestudytools.com/blogs/association-of-biblical-counselors/victory-over-the-shame-of-sexual-abuse.html.

2. Marcus Bockmuehl, *The Epistle to the Philippians* (London: A&C Black, 1997), 62.

About the Author

Sheila Walsh grew up in Scotland and is known as "the encourager" to the over 6 million women she's met and spoken to around the world. She loves being a Bible teacher, making God's Word practical, and sharing her own story of how God met her when she was at her lowest point and lifted her up again.

Her message: GOD IS FOR YOU!

Sheila loves writing and has sold more than five million books. She is also the cohost of the television program *Life Today*, airing in the US, Canada, Europe, and Australia with over 300 million viewers daily.

Calling Texas home, Sheila lives in Dallas with her husband, Barry; her son, Christian; and three little dogs—Belle, Tink, and Maggie.

You can stay in touch with her on Facebook at sheilawalshconnects, on Twitter at @sheilawalsh, and on Instagram at sheilawalsh1.

SheilaWalsh.com

Visit Sheila online

to subscribe to her **newsletter**,
read her **blog**, and learn more
about **Wednesdays in the Word**!

SheilaWalsh1

SheilaWalshConnects

SheilaWalsh

Watch Sheila!

Each week on
Wednesdays in the Word,

Sheila Walsh shares insights and revelation from the Bible as she studies God's Word and discusses what He has put on her heart.

VISIT

SheilaWalsh.com/watch-sheila

OR

LifeToday.org